ॐ▲

THE NINE FREEDOMS

by
George King, D.D., Th.D.

REVISED EDITION

The Aetherius Press
LOS ANGELES • FOUNDED 1955 • LONDON

First Published
1963

Second Impression
May, 1974

Third Impression
January, 2001

Fourth Impression
August, 2011

Fifth Impression
January, 2019

The Nine Freedoms is printed and published by The Aetherius
Press, 6202 Afton Place, Hollywood, California 90028-8298,
U.S.A.
(323) 465-9652   www.aetherius.org   info@aetherius.org

Printed in the United States of America

DEDICATION

This book is dedicated to that Cosmic Adept known simply as Mars Sector 6, Who, in compassion for humanity, gave the Mystic Text at this most significant time in the history of Earth.

FOREWORD

In 1961, an ancient and wise Cosmic Intelligence, code-named Mars Sector 6, saw fit to deliver the most profound spiritual philosophy the world had ever received. It was called The Nine Freedoms. Since then, thousands of people have had their lives completely changed by coming into contact with this extraordinary series of Teachings. I know—I am one of them.

I have made a point of studying the philosophies of many religions, and have found wisdom in all of them. Much of their teaching is still as valid today as it was when it was first delivered. But The Nine Freedoms goes further—it continues where they end. It is even more relevant now than it was when it was first delivered and it will be still more relevant in the future. It is a work of timeless wisdom designed specifically for the New Age which is now dawning.

Reverend Charles Abrahamson's *Introduction to the Author* gives an excellent insight into Doctor King's exceptional achievements up to the delivery of The Nine Freedoms. After this, Doctor King's work continued unabated from Mission to Mission, and teaching to teaching, until his demise in 1997. To the best of my knowledge, there is simply no one else who has even claimed to be in regular contact with Interplanetary Masters for anything like the same period of over 43 years.

The authenticity of this claim, I believe, is confirmed by the otherworldly calibre of the knowledge Doctor King brought to the Earth. A subjective view, you might think, but there have been objective results for the thousands who have discovered, as a result, greater enlightenment, a more purposeful life and above all the ability to make a real difference in the world. And if, like me, you encounter cynicism about such things all too frequently, you too will find the antidote for this in The Nine Freedoms.

The style of Mars Sector 6, Who has been described by other Masters as a Lord of Karma, is superbly concise, yet resonant with meaning. As well as studying the texts you would be advised to contemplate deeply on them one by one. Each Freedom is introduced by a prominent and wise Ascended Master from this Earth known as Saint Goo-Ling. There is also a beautiful Transmission by that great Master of Love, Jesus, Who came from the Planet Venus.

Doctor King's commentaries at the end of each text are truly brilliant, even when compared with, say, the mystical perceptions on the I-Ching by Confucius or the penetrating analysis of Patanjali's Aphorisms by Swami Vivekananda. With his hallmark of down-to-earth practicality, blended with a clear explanation of even the most advanced concepts, Doctor King gives us a treasure of knowledge at the end of each Freedom.

It is a privilege for me to write the Foreword to this edition, which is more than a book or even a bible—it is the ultimate signpost on the road to human evolution.

Dr. Richard Lawrence

Executive Secretary, European Headquarters
The Aetherius Society

London, England
November, 2000

INTRODUCTION TO THE AUTHOR

Doctor George King

Doctor George King was born in Wellington, Shropshire, England, on January 23rd, 1919. Very early in life his deep Spiritual interests found expression in orthodox Christianity. But it was only a matter of time before he became convinced that there was more to life than that shown to the orthodox. While still very young, he began to study psychic phenomena. This research was characterized by the intense determination and drive which has become so familiar to all who know him. It quickly carried him deep beneath the fascinating superficial strata to the causes of this phenomena, which he could clearly understand.

Through the exacting use of discrimination and detachment, the passing years brought Doctor King such familiarity with paranormal phenomena that it became virtually impossible for him to be deceived or misled. The "fairyland" of visions, psychic sights and sounds which hold most researchers prisoners to their enchantments, remained to him a laboratory in which precise laws and formulas held. He began to demonstrate his psychic abilities which, by now, had become acutely developed. Within a short time he had successfully and repeatedly demonstrated all psychic powers then commonly known.

Dissatisfied, Doctor King believed that there was yet more to be wrested from the complicated and engrossing field of applied Metaphysics. He began to practice Yoga. Again his concentrated, driving effort quickly led him deep beneath the surface levels into the secrets of this true science. Increased awareness and ability came. He soon arrived at a stage where his mastery of terrestrial phenomena placed him completely above it, in a position where he could never become obsessed or used by it in ignorance.

In the year 1954, Doctor King was deeply engrossed in Spiritual Healing. Research on the higher planes, with the assistance of the intelligences there, was only one of his methods. Conscious projection into the higher realms in order to learn the deep Metaphysical Truths led him through a series of advanced Initiations. Unsuspectingly he was ready for another great step forward.

When in 1954 the well-known "Command" was received from Higher Authority to prepare himself to become the voice of Interplanetary Parliament, he was shocked by the implications of the statement. The method of communication was not unfamiliar and there was no uncertainty about the authority of the Being Who had commanded him. Shortly afterwards, Doctor King was visited in his own home by a famous Master whom he knew to be alive and active in India at the time. Although the contact was in every way physical, the Master entered and left through a locked door which he did not open. During this meeting, Doctor King was given further information about the "Command" and instructions as to what his next steps would be. Through a series of highly specialized exercises, especially devised for the purpose, he quickly learned to bring about that elevated state of consciousness which is absolutely necessary to the establishment of mental rapport with the Beings Who inhabit the other Planets. He mastered the science of Raja, Gnani and Kundalini Yoga until he could consciously attain the state of Samadhi. It was then that the Cosmic Masters of the Solar System began using Doctor King as Primary Terrestrial Mental Channel.

In the following years Doctor King abandoned all business interests and materialistic ambitions as the information from the Space Intelligences grew in importance, seriousness and urgency. On Their direction he founded an international Metaphysical Order called The Aetherius Society. He began publishing a regular magazine called *Cosmic Voice*, lectured widely throughout England and continued to serve frequently as the mental channel for numerous Transmissions from advanced Cosmic Intelligences while in deep Samadhic trance before hundreds of people.

Scores of radio, television and press interviews were given and it is significant to note that never once was any inconsistency noted in the story of his vast experience. It was not long before public interest caused him to become the first person ever to demonstrate Yogic Samadhi over television, under the glaring lights of the British

Broadcasting Corporation, so that a Cosmic Master from another Planet could actually speak to Britain! This unique and historic event occurred on May 21st, 1959 and was broadcast to an estimated viewing audience of several million. This programme proved so popular that it has been re-broadcast again and again through the ensuing years.

Still operating from his headquarters in England, Doctor George King entered the deep mystic state known as Cosmic Consciousness through a controlled and conscious rise of the power of Kundalini. His description of this exalted state in Chapter 5 of *The Nine Freedoms*, leaves no question as to its true nature or that he had, in fact, entered it. The eye, guiding the hand which painted this living picture was fixed, not upon any pale copy, but upon the scene itself —we need no experts to tell us this. This chapter, taken alone, bestows a rare greatness upon the book, for it reveals, in part, the greatness of the author.

While still in England, Doctor King was summoned by Cosmic Intelligences to an audience on a mighty Spacecraft then hovering above Earth. While there he was privileged to be allowed to actually witness the elevated Initiation of Ascension. He returned from this unique and majestic event with the implicit instructions to relate his experiences to mankind. Thus was he the first Yogi Adept ever to be entrusted with the responsibility of reporting the ceremony of an actual Initiation of Ascension performed in Space, by a Cosmic Master.

In "The Glory Of Ascension," in Chapter 6 of this book, Doctor King gives us a brilliant narration of a great event and also clearly shows the relationship, cooperation and close liaison between terrestrial and Solar Hierarchies.

Quite suddenly and almost simultaneously, two great Missions were handed to him. He was given the tremendous responsibility of serving as the mental channel through whom the Venusian we know as the Master Jesus delivered "The Twelve Blessings," an extension of that Great Being's Sermon on the Mount to include a Cosmic concept. At the same time he began the titanic job of performing "Operation Starlight," which the Masters have called: "The most important single Metaphysical task ever undertaken upon Earth in this, Her present life."

Acting upon direct instructions from Cosmic Authority, Doctor King came to the United States in 1959. During the next three years he travelled and lectured extensively through America, Australia and Europe, performing the separate phases of "Operation Starlight" as they fell due, on 18 mountains throughout the world.

Doctor King again publicly demonstrated Yogic Samadhi before audiences sometimes numbering two thousand. Again, this time in Los Angeles, he served as the mental channel for a stirring message to the people of Earth from a Cosmic Being before the television cameras of KCOP-TV, Channel 13, on "The Tom Duggan Show," on July 19th, 1960.

"Operation Starlight" was not yet completed when, in 1961, the Masters announced that yet another specialized series of Transmissions must be delivered through Doctor George King. These Transmissions were given and are here published as *The Nine Freedoms*.

Such, to date, has been the preparation, experience and life of the man whose Missions—already so vast in scope as to be almost beyond endurance—culminated in the added responsibility of being chosen by the Cosmic Masters Themselves as the mental channel and custodian of "The Nine Freedoms."

Reverend Charles E. Abrahamson

CONTENTS

ILLUSTRATIONS

INTRODUCTION

For thousands of years thinking man has looked aloft into the mighty vastness of the heavens and has asked:

"Do I ever leave this Earth? Where do I go? How do I get there?"

Deeply intrigued he has searched through physics, philosophy and orthodox Religions for these answers—but, for the most part, he has searched in vain. Some creeds have even forbidden him to ask, to search further. But the brave, ignoring the threats of hell and damnation, have continued their struggles to find the answers to the most baffling questions which have ever faced humanity.

Some more daring souls have studied the mystic and occult sciences in search of their answers. They have plodded from the séance rooms to the occult tomes which tried, in extremely verbose language, to give them an acceptable definition of life and its eventual destination. Yet, even the most erudite of these works have not given the seeker a plain, easily understandable answer to all these foremost questions. Even a most carefully prepared precis of the known philosophies of the East and West has not provided the full answers to these three questions. Always there has been a part of the answer missing—as though purposely shrouded in some strange mystery.

Why is this so? Because until now, man has, by design, been cut off from the full Truth, has not been given an easily understandable path through his future. By design he has not been informed of the essential stopping places on his long road through Evolution.

You may ask: "By whose design has this vital information been kept from me? If at last these secrets are revealed—why is this Revelation given now?"

In order to answer these questions it is necessary to go back into the past—back before the days of the Ancient Brahmins and the Chinese, back before the time when man started to write his history in the Akashic records of Earth.

Here is the history of man—your history.

Hundreds of thousands of years ago there was another Planet in this Solar System. This Planet made an orbit between Mars and Jupiter. It was a small mass about the size of Earth. A green prosperous world inhabited by a people who were, for the most part, reasonably satisfied with their progression. This civilization had not reached a state of really advanced culture, but had nevertheless attained a stage which afforded an abundance of necessities which made life comparatively comfortable for all.

These people had likes and dislikes, hopes and ambitions as indeed do you. Male and female caused procreation of the races as do the people on Earth.

They studied the philosophies and dabbled in the sciences as do terrestrials, except that these people were more advanced in many ways than are earthlings. The Planet was so highly mechanized that robots took care of all the menial tasks. The inhabitants had discovered a rudimentary form of Space travel, but soon found that their craft did not possess sufficient cruising range owing to the fact that their fuel was too heavy to allow them to penetrate far into the System. They could control their weather so that drought and famine became long forgotten. The majority, having an abundance of food, having no menial tasks to perform soon became content to while away their unrecallable hours in the sun. They became, in comparison with the higher Planetary cultures, a selfish, lackadaisical people seeking after their own enjoyment, as do the majority of terrestrials.

Then the disease came.

It probably started subtly in the minds of those few men of science who shunned the procrastinating majority, in a fervent search for material conquest, thus leaving themselves open to the incurable affliction.

The mental disease manifested itself as a lust for greater power.

They found it!

They exploded a hydrogen bomb and completely destroyed the Planet Maldek and murdered the whole populace in one blinding flash of searing flame.

Not the hydrogen isotope bomb which only releases one ten thousandth part of its force as does the murder weapon on Earth, but the scientists of Maldek discovered how to convert hydrogen mass into energy in its entirety and thus murdered a whole world. All that is now left of that beautiful green Planet, which at one time teemed with life, gaining its expression through experience, is the asteroid belt. Thousands of pieces of cold rock, spinning through Space, lifeless, devoid of atmosphere, a burned, broken, dead world.

Although the terrible disease, the lust for power and material conquest, affected only a few, the majority of people were so lackadaisical, so confined to their own petty contentment and ease of life that they allowed this horrible Cosmic crime to be committed. They were all just as responsible for this terrible sin as were the few who actually caused it.

The millions of lifestreams who inhabited Maldek were suddenly released on to their different etheric planes. According to the perfect Law of Karma, these lifestreams had to reincarnate again, under strict limitation, upon another Planet in the Solar System. They could not reincarnate upon Jupiter, because even in those days, the inhabitants had reached such a high state of Spiritual culture that the Planet was used as a reception centre for the Interplanetary Confederation, which actually had its seat upon Saturn. Jupiter, with its massive bulk, approximately 630 times the size of Earth, could well accommodate the thousands of representatives coming from different worlds within and even outside of the Solar System to the seat of learning— Saturn. They could not be reincarnated upon Uranus or Venus because both these peoples had reached such a high state of culture that the involved intelligences from Maldek would not have learned the lessons essential to their further progress. Mercury was already operating as the major communications centre for the Solar System. Mars was already inhabited by an advanced race who were the engineers and builders in the Solar System.

The Earth was approached.

The Cosmic Hierarchy first made an appeal to the Earth as an Intelligence, to see if She would agree to withhold Her Evolutionary progress and bear the limitations which would be necessarily imposed upon Her should the people from Maldek be allowed to reincarnate.

The Earth, being a great Planetary Lord, took merciful compassion upon the killers of Maldek and agreed to their reincarnation upon Her back and thereby agreed to the thousands of years of necessary limitation, which would have to be imposed during their reincarnation, so that they could gain essential experience.

The Cosmic Hierarchy then approached the true inhabitants of Earth, a highly cultured race of individuals called—Adamic man. Adamic man agreed that he would give place to the reincarnating lifestreams and he cooperated in such a manner as to make this cycle of incarnation complete.

Gradually those too lazy to stop the shocking Cosmic crime of the destruction of Maldek and those who had actually brought it about, were reincarnated upon Earth. Adamic man stayed for a time giving instruction, guidance and help to the mutants which plagued the grass of Earth. Then, eventually, when Adamic man had caused some semblance of civilization to be brought into being on Earth, he, obeying his instructions according to the Law, left the human race to its own devices.

Out of the gross limitation of atomic mutation the civilization of Lemuria dragged its weary self. It grew in culture. The Earth became somewhat similar to what Maldek had been. The people began to probe the philosophies and the sciences again. The Earth gave of Its abundance and the Lemurian civilization flourished.

In its hey-day, it was a civilization of much finer culture than we know on Earth today. The Lemurians established a liaison between themselves and the Planets, Venus and Mars. The Venusians and Martians, not dictating in anyway to the Lemurians, nevertheless taught them many lessons.

But alas, the disease struck again.

Lemuria was split into two different camps, the White Magicians and the evil black magicians. The White Magicians, learning many things from the Visitors from other Planets had advanced greatly in Metaphysical sciences. The black magicians probed the atom. Again, for the second time, they unlocked the forces within God's tiny building blocks and destroyed the civilization of Lemuria.

But this time those people who were ready were actually evacuated prior to the destruction of Lemuria by vehicles from other Planets which landed upon Earth in order to perform this evacuation. In fact, even the evil forces were warned time and time again of their folly, but alas they took no notice and died as a result.

Again those left were born through gross limitation on and off a world seething with radio-active poisoning until, eventually, after thousands of years, another semblance of a culture came into being and slowly at first, then later gaining momentum, the civilization of Atlantis flourished upon Earth. Again space travel was established. Again some listened to the voice of Wisdom coming from Higher Sources and there was a split into three definite camps. The few, searching for a force to give them conquest over the whole Solar System, the majority not caring much, because they were content to live in their procrastinations and the other few, who had proved themselves ready for the higher teachings and possessed the logic and faith to accept the voice of Higher Authority. There was a great mental battle on Atlantis between the White Magicians and the evil practitioners of the black arts. Again the sadistic minds of the dark ones unlocked the pandora's box and invented two atomic weapons. They quarrelled among themselves. One side made a weapon called "Indra's dart," which was an atomic bomb, and the other side invented a controllable atomic ray called—surprisingly enough, "The Brahma weapon" or "weapon of God."

Now the Martians, who had been in close liaison with the White Magicians on Atlantis, saw that a great war was brewing between the two evil factions and landed five large Spacecraft upon Earth called, "Cities of Shan."

The White Magicians, and indeed all those who were ready for evacuation just prior to the outbreak of atomic war, were taken off the Earth. The evil forces, beset with greed and lust for material supremacy, warred with each other. As neither side could win such an atomic war—down fell the civilization of Atlantis into charred radio-active ruins.

It is a strange thing that, if this Truth were written as a novel, no one would ever accept it to be in anyway feasible or logical. No thinking man would believe that a race of intelligent people could, three times in succession, make the same mistake, although twice previously they had been forced to suffer gross limitation for this very mistake. No humanitarian would ever believe, were this written as fiction, that people could have been so absurdly foolish as the people upon Earth have been.

But, believe it or not, this is a brief resume of what is written in the always truthful Akashic records.

So much for the past—what about today?

Again the forces of the atom have been unleashed. Again the world is divided against itself. Again we stand in a similar position to the one we occupied before the destruction of Maldek, before the destruction of Lemuria. We stand in a similar position now, as you read this, to the one we stood in before the atomic destruction of Atlantis.

It should also be noted that after the destruction of Lemuria the Cosmic Hierarchy saw fit to place a barrier around the Earth called, in some occult books, "the ring-pass not." In physical terms this barrier is called—the ionosphere. After the destruction of Atlantis "the ring-pass not," or ionosphere, was greatly intensified. This intensification tended to cut man off from the higher forms of inspiration as a well-deserved limitation, making advancement so much more difficult for him. This move had to be brought about according to Karmic Law. But it should also be appreciated that both in Atlantean and modern times, man has always had access to the philosophies and the definitions of the Divine Laws. In modern times, this access was made possible through the Wisdom propounded by Interplanetary Avatars such as Shri Krishna, Buddha, Patanjali, the Master Jesus, who came to Earth to teach and in the case of the latter, to die to save terrestrials from a catastrophe. Mankind, even in his darkest hour, has never been left alone. He chose to disregard the teachings of the Great Ones, thereby exercising his petty freewill which has led him into the troubles which he has faced.

This is a very brief history of why man is here upon Earth and why he is at the bottom of the Evolutionary ladder in this Solar System. No other peoples in the Solar System have committed the worst possible crime, namely that of murdering a Planetary Intelligence.

Maldek, referred to in some Holy Works as—the angel which fell out of heaven, was the place from whence you came to this Earth. To refer back to the question, "By whose design has the vital information regarding man's eventual Evolution been kept from him?" Who else has designed the withholding of this information except man himself by his gross disobedience to the Divine Laws.

To refer back to the other question: "If at last these secrets are revealed—why is this Revelation given now?"

Now, mankind stands in, to quote Higher Authority: "The valley of decision."

He has to decide whether or not he will bring about those conditions which will destroy modern civilization through another atomic war, or whether he will spare himself this suffering. The key to man's future virtually lies in his own hands. These are the last days of the old order. The New Order for mankind will be surer Peace—deeper joy— more lasting prosperity than he has ever known before, conditions will be so good upon this Earth as to be beyond his wildest imaginings, or he can re-live the terrors of Maldek, Lemuria and Atlantis— which ever he likes.

Although mankind stands today in a position similar to that before Maldek was destroyed, there is one major difference between the two situations and that is this: the Supreme Lords of Karma have now declared, in such a way that this Declaration is irrevocable and cannot in any way be changed by any Power in the Solar System, that under no account will the Planet Itself be destroyed. If man chooses to debase his energy by engaging in war he will then leave the Earth, through death, to be born again upon another Planet.

The Lords have declared that the great Millenium of Peace and Enlightenment must come, but only those who have expended the necessary efforts to learn the Divine Law and have fashioned their lives within the framework of its lasting Truth, will be left upon the Earth. For only such as these will deserve to enjoy this new, wonderful age. It must be understood that the Karmic Lords have made this Declaration not so much because of mankind, but out of consideration for the great Goddess known as Earth. She has suffered Her limitations long enough and the shackles She had to impose upon Herself, in order to make a Space Refuge for man, will be taken off shortly. Just as Jesus suffered upon the cross for a certain measurable length of time, so also has the suffering of this Earth been measured exactly and soon Her limitations will be dispensed with and the great Cosmic Initiation of Earth will take place. It is prior to this supreme Cosmic event, this last sorting of the wheat from the chaff on Earth, that the mystic text known as *The Nine Freedoms* has been given to man in such a way that, if he thinks at all, he can read and understand it. It is because man stands today upon the verge of the most important happenings in his total history that these Revelations have been made by the Higher Powers so that, even in the eleventh hour of man's decision, the answers to the most outstanding questions which have baffled him for centuries have now been given.

The Nine Freedoms, as a signpost to the future Evolution of humanity, has been given at this time so that those who are ready may learn how to progress bravely into the Millenium of Peace on Earth—then later through the Cosmos.

GEORGE KING, D.D.

This Mystic Text is as a wise
all-knowing Light which will guide you
from the Karmic confines of earth
through glorious Ascension
into lasting Freedom

CHAPTER 1

THE FIRST FREEDOM WILL BE BRAVERY

SAINT GOO-LING

"The Operation known as The Nine Freedoms will be given.

"The organizers must procure small wooden Crosses which will be Blessed and given to each attender after Ninth time.

"This Operation is specifically designed to be of help to you all.

"The Freedoms, as with 'The Twelve Blessings,' may not be necessarily delivered in strict order of importance, but in the order which allows certain Power to be radiated at specific time.

"Some of greatest pronouncements made to Earth just lately have been made by Cosmic Being known as—Mars Sector 6. This Intelligence will give The Nine Freedoms.

"Be silent everyone, do not shuffle, for this is important Operation.

"I go."

MARS SECTOR 6

"This is Mars Sector 6 pronouncing—The Nine Freedoms.

"The First Freedom will be—BRAVERY.

"BRAVERY is essential in all things, for while the aspirant allows the negative accumulation of fear to discolour his outlook, he cannot ever truly aspire to Freedom.

"Freedom from fear can be brought into active manifestation within all men providing they have knowledge. Knowledge of the right kind dispels fear, whether the manifestation of this fear be petty or more potent.

"It is not necessary for man upon Terra to fear man upon Terra, for if you obey the Unchangeable Laws, indeed by your obedience do you burn fear in the bright light of dawning Enlightenment.

"Man upon Terra today is beset by strange fears which imprison his actions, his very outlook; which imprison his mind—aye, even his psychic abilities.

"Fear is a weapon being now used by the darkest forces to cause you to become their ignorant pawns.

"Break away from this fear by delving deep within yourself and discovering the great dormant Powers which are latent there.

"Break away from this tight bondage by so Enlightening yourselves that this weapon may be rendered useless.

"Study fear for what it is. Study it coldly without emotion. You will discover that it is but a state of mind which you have formulated for yourselves.

"This state of mind is the result of Karma, environment and present outlook.

"Karma—you can, at this very moment, make for yourself a Karmic pattern which, when manifested, will not bring vague fear as a result.

"You can rise above environment, for it is a changing thing, it is not real.

"Knowledge gained by adherence to the Unchangeable Laws can bring to you that stage of Enlightenment which dispels fear. A state of mind can be changed at once for good or for evil. It is just as easy to have a state of mind unclouded by fear as it is to allow it to be warped by this intrusion.

"Have this outlook upon Life. Act in this way and fear becomes non-existent.

"When fear has been transmuted in the fires of applied knowledge, tempered by Love, you become Wise. In your Wisdom there is fortitude and BRAVERY.

"The First Freedom—dispel fear. Go forth into BRAVERY and you will know many things, for you will have taken an essential step upon the ladder of Evolution.

"There will come a day when you will be examined in this Light. Prepare for tomorrow's examination now and Mastery will be yours.

"Know this: the tests which now confront you terrestrials have had to be so designed in order to give you essential experience.

"BRAVERY is victory through experience.

"Be Brave, not foolish; but Brave through Wisdom—and know The First Freedom.

"Transmissions now discontinued."

Delivered on Sunday, February 12th, 1961.

BRAVERY

In order to understand the deeper Metaphysical Truths contained within The Nine Freedoms, it is necessary to examine certain passages from the text. The passages which are analyzed in the commentary have been carefully chosen so that as much vital information as possible can be passed on to the serious Metaphysical student. Even so, it should be pointed out, that every sentence which makes up the text of The Nine Freedoms should be subjected to close study by the student, whether or not it has been treated to commentary by the author. The motive which prompted the Cosmic Master, Mars Sector 6, to deliver this outstanding text was to effect a rise of consciousness in the genuine student, who is not only trying to evolve himself, but has, rightly, a deep yearning for some definite statement from Higher Authority regarding his eventual Evolutionary destination in the Cosmos. Once the student has recognized the wondrous glories which are, to him, a possible attainment, he will discover an even greater yearning to progress and a stronger power of endurance, which will enable this long, but rewarding journey through Evolution to be made.

These are the main reasons which prompted the author to prepare the following commentary on the mystical text of The Nine Freedoms.

"The Operation known as The Nine Freedoms will be given."
The implication behind this commencing statement by Saint Goo-Ling is that The Nine Freedoms was a definite Metaphysical Manipulation of Power. Exactly what type of energy was radiated, during the time that the instruction called The Nine Freedoms was given, will be seen a little later on in the text.

"The organizers must procure small wooden Crosses."
These wooden Crosses were later Blessed, charged with vibrant energy and were given to every member of the invited audience who attended The Nine Freedoms. Later in the text by Saint Goo-Ling, another reference was made to The Freedoms, that They may not be necessarily delivered in strict order of importance, but in the order which allows a certain Power to be radiated at a specific time. This is another suggestion that this was a definite manipulation of Power, as well as an Operation of Metaphysical education.

The Nine Freedoms are steps upon the ladder of Evolution, essential steps which every man upon Earth must take in order to gain a highly elevated Cosmic status.

"The First Freedom will be—BRAVERY.
"BRAVERY is essential in all things, for while the aspirant allows the negative accumulation of fear to discolour his outlook, he cannot ever truly aspire to Freedom."

The more we think about the implications behind this statement, the more we are sure that it is correct. When man leaves the well-trodden path of orthodoxy and genuinely tries to bring the more highly elevated mystic states about within himself, he must pass through periods of great misery and depression, as well as phases of elation and deep joy. He also must pass through experiences which put his Bravery to the supreme test. There are many upon this path who have fallen back through fear, when they have been virtually standing upon the very brink of some elevated Metaphysical illumination. The first time that true Meditation is brought about and the aspirant is able to look through, what is termed in the west, the Christ Centre, he is absolutely stricken with awe. Many aspirants stop at this particular state making no effort to approach it again, because of their fear. A man fears that which he cannot understand. He cannot be expected to understand an elevated state unless he is familiar with it. Unfamiliarity brings fear, if allowed to do so. Therefore, Bravery is doubly essential. It is the first definite step that we must take upon the ladder of Evolution into the true study of the Cosmic Science of Being.

In this text the statement is made that, man cannot truly aspire to Enlightenment or Freedom, which is one and the same thing, without being brave enough to do so. In deep Meditation, the first vision through the psychic centre within the forehead causes the student to feel that he is no longer of this Earth. He feels that he is above the Earth, detached from it, completely alone in the Cosmos. Such Illumination as this affects some students in much the same way that the light of the Sun would affect a man blind from birth, who gazed right into the dazzling orb for the first time after suddenly being given the power of sight. Many aspirants have been so terrified during this experience, that they have stopped where they were, or have left the straight, stony path for the more basic types of psychic phenomena (Note 1). This is one of the important lessons to be learned and no man will go any further in his Evolution, until he has learned to be brave enough to overcome all of his personal and petty fears.

Knowledge of the right kind dispels fear. Mankind is fearful of the things about which he knows nothing. If he thoroughly understands a phenomena, he becomes fearless of it, even though he might be very careful of it. For instance, when a man learns that poison will kill him, he will no longer drink it, because his knowledge tells him that it is detrimental to his health, but not because he fears it.

"It is not necessary for man upon Terra to fear man upon Terra, for if you obey the Unchangeable Laws, indeed by your obedience do you burn fear in the bright light of dawning Enlightenment."

It is not necessary for man to fear man, or country to fear country. If there were one single country upon this Earth today which strictly adhered to the teachings of Jesus, Buddha, Shri Krishna, or to any of the other true Cosmic teachings which have been given to Earth, that country would not only stand alone, would not only outshine every other country in the world, but could be completely fearless in its dealings with every other country throughout the Earth.

If this were a true Christian world, then we would not need to have the big armies, the navies and the devastating atom bombs which threaten to annihilate civilization. Weapons are made by people who are fearful of one another, by people who do not understand the Unchangeable Laws of the Universe. All weapons, especially the atomic bomb, are the direct result of ignorance, not Enlightenment. The Enlightened man does not need to protect himself with deadly weapons, for he knows that their use is against the Great Laws as laid down by the Master Jesus, by the Master Buddha and other great Beings. He knows that his true protective Power lies in his Enlightenment and not in his ability to maim and even murder his fellowmen.

It seems that even the basic laws of man these days are built upon fear. If you perform an action contrary to these laws, such and such a punishment will be handed out. The Enlightened man knows that he has no right to inflict any punishment upon any man. He knows that virtually every man is learning, including himself. Enlightenment, knowledge and adherence to the Unchangeable Laws of the Universe dispel fear. They make a man brave enough to stand, if necessary, completely alone in the midst of his fellowmen and still be unafraid to declare himself or to live his beliefs.

There are many lives of difference between the ordinary fearful man, who feels he must protect himself with devastating murder weapons and the advanced, Enlightened man, who can face life bravely and fearlessly, can look life straight in the face because of his greater knowledge of life, because he is more aware of where he has been and of his eventual destination.

"Fear is a weapon now being used by the darkest forces to cause you to become their ignorant pawns."

Fear is the most powerful weapon of the darkest forces. If fear did not exist the dark forces would not be so powerful, because their very lifelines would be dissected. The dark forces, which are active in this world now, are those intelligences on the lower astral realms who are able to impress a pawn like "hitler" to cause division in the world. Fear is the result of terrestrial division and while evil entities can impress any one to cause division, their own force becomes stronger and their position more sure. The fearless, Enlightened man cannot be so impressed. He cannot ever become a whimpering pawn, trembling in the hands of some sadistic black magician. Eventually he can become a wise Buddha or a gentle Jesus, but never a quaking, fearful "hitler."

You are advised to break away from fear by delving deep within yourself and discovering the dormant Powers which are latent there.

"Study fear for what it is. Study it coldly, without emotion. You will discover that it is but a state of mind which you have formulated for yourselves."

Fear is only a state of mind of man's own making and because he has made it, he can very easily change it. It is a warped mental creation and as such it can be transmuted by the very brain which created this mutation. It can be changed into a higher state of consciousness, which is more positive, more lasting, which is capable of regarding fear as an unnecessary and even an evil intruder.

Fear can be transmuted by Enlightenment, which can be brought about by discovering the latent Powers within and bringing these into active manifestation on Earth. Later on in the text we are told exactly how to do this.

"This state of mind is a result of Karma, environment and present outlook. Karma—you can at this very moment make for your-

*self a Karmic pattern which, when manifested will not bring vague
fear as a result."*

All Creation is governed strictly by the all-pervasive Law of Karma.
No aspect of Creation is outside of this Law. It is a perfect, irrevocable Law, for it is one of the Laws, Which are God. Thousands of words
have been written about the Law of Karma and yet it can be
explained simply and briefly. In reference to the Law of Karma, the
Lord Buddha stated that: "Action and reaction are opposite and equal."
The Master Jesus referred to it in this way: "As you sow, so shall you
reap." Note, "so shall you reap,"—not, so may you reap. The Law of
Karma is perfectly fair and absolutely just. According to your action,
you reap the repercussion or reaction, about this there can be no
doubt. This Law is one of the Inevitables in Creation. If you live a life
which demands a good reaction, then rest assured that this good
reaction will come to you; if not in this life, then in the next one. If,
on the other hand, you live a life which demands a painful reaction,
then rest assured that this type of reaction will come, either in the
present life or in the next one. There is no doubt about this. The Law
of Karma is not theory; it is logical, basic fact. It is one of the most pronounced Laws and in its wider framework, one of the most easily
understandable Laws. Today is the tomorrow that you made for yourselves yesterday. No man, no matter whether he be commoner or king,
can escape this and no man has ever done so. Even the shining Stars,
perceived in the vast firmaments above us, are just as confined within
the framework of this Law as are the microbes on Earth, called men.

Because man has virtually created his present Karmic pattern, he
can and indeed does, change this pattern from hour to hour and even
minute to minute. The text states that fear is a result of Karma, environment and present outlook. The Karma we can alter whenever we
choose to do so. One thing is certain that by our right actions of the
present we can control our future Karma (Note 2).

*"You can rise above environment, for it is a changing thing, it is
not real."*

Nothing which changes can be real. Reality is unchangeability.
Therefore, anything which changes is not reality. Environment can be
risen above. How many times has history proven this beyond any
doubt? A child, setting off along the road of life, born in slum conditions, without any education, lacking even the necessary parental

care and love so necessary, has many times become a person of renown and distinction. Whereas, others given the finest education, the most tender loving care in early childhood, have failed to distinguish themselves in the field of human endeavor. We know that whenever we choose to rise above our environment, we can do so.

Present outlook is also something which we can change immediately. The text declares that a state of mind can be changed at once for good or evil. We all know this to be true. If we want to be pessimistic, now, even as we read this, we can make ourselves so. If we want to be optimistic, we can change at once to a hopeful frame of mind. Therefore, present outlook is something which is entirely the product of each individual (Note 3).

So, fear in man is caused by Karma, environment and present outlook. We can control our Karma, we can rise above our environment and we can change our present outlook. Therefore, every man has within himself the ability to overcome fear, to change it into Bravery and make a very definite, decisive step forward in his climb up the ladder of Evolution.

"When fear has been transmuted in the fires of acquired knowledge, tempered by Love, you become Wise. In your Wisdom there is fortitude and BRAVERY."

If we carefully apply the knowledge given to us in this text, we can rise above many of our limitations, dispelling fear and then be prepared to meet our tomorrow bravely, realizing full well that we have made for ourselves a wonderful future.

"There will come a day when you will be examined in this Light. Prepare for tomorrow's examination now and Mastery will be yours."

The reference here, "examined in this Light," is most important. It is not put in by chance and it means exactly what it says. Once a great Truth, such as this one, has been given to mankind, from that time on, man is completely responsible for applying this knowledge to his mind and if it appears to be logical, acting upon it.

When Mars Sector 6 states that: *"You will be examined in this Light,"* He undoubtedly means just that. A day comes to each and every man when he must go to the Hall of self judgment. Not to appear as a wretched prisoner before some cruel judge, who delights in bringing before him his numerous faults and condemning him for them, but before a Cosmic Being, Who instructs him how to judge himself. This he will do. His Higher Consciousness will see what lessons are absolutely essential and will arrange a reincarnation into a set of conditions which will allow these lessons to be learned.

In our study of The Nine Freedoms, we are starting a well-planned journey into an aspect of the greatest Wisdom ever given to mankind, for it is vitally important to the world as a whole in this stage of Evolution. It is the text upon which will be based the examination papers of the future. No one will ever read this text by chance, but everyone who does read it will be responsible to their own higher conscience for abiding by the Laws herein as far as they are humanly able.

When in the Hall of self judgment, no man, who has come into contact with these Teachings, will be able to make the excuse that he did not know the Law. The statement: *"You will be examined in this Light,"* occurs several times throughout the whole mystic text of The Nine Freedoms and it is undoubtedly one of the most important statements ever made. It is a definite pointer to the future. It is as though the Intelligence Who gave this text had such compassion upon mortal man that He went out of His way to warn him to take these Teachings so seriously that, when his inevitable examination comes after physical death, he would not fail on too many points.

"Prepare for tomorrow's examination this day and Mastery will be yours."
Highly significant words and they mean exactly what they say.

"Know this: the tests which now confront you terrestrials have had to be so designed in order to give you essential experience."
Mankind has proven that he needs the present tests and experiences through which he is now living. Had he lived his former lives correctly, he would only have attracted to himself conditions which would have brought great joy and achievements far beyond those he can now realize. This knowledge alone should make you realize the importance of adhering to the lasting aspects of Wisdom, of which The First Freedom is undoubtedly one of the most important. For we are reminded that: *"BRAVERY is victory through experience,"* and it is up to us all to live through this experience correctly and so take the first step upon the ladder of true, lasting joy towards our re-discovered Cosmic Status.

AUTHOR'S RECOMMENDATIONS

NOTE 1. Study *Light On The Path*, for further clarification of the state referred to. This book is published by the Theosophical Society.

NOTE 2. A study of the specially devised Metaphysical lesson, *Karma And Reincarnation*, will give students a deeper insight into this subject.

NOTE 3. Study the Metaphysical lesson, *Man's Mind*, for further information regarding the function and control of your mental abilities.

The last two recommended lessons are obtainable from the publishers of *The Nine Freedoms*.

CHAPTER 2

THE SECOND FREEDOM WILL BE LOVE

SAINT GOO-LING
"Next time Prasad will be offered to all who come.
"Know that, during The Second Freedom, much Power will be released to all world. Many here will be used as channels for this Power, relax, let Power flow through you out to world. No need even to guide it, for will be manipulated by Higher Forces.
"I go."

MARS SECTOR 6
"This is Mars Sector 6.
"The Second Freedom will be—LOVE.
"Upon Terra this word is wrongly used. LOVE is not the measure of emotion, whether soft or violent, it is something deeper, something greater, something which cannot be measured even in mind conception.
"LOVE is an all permeating energy which is above mind. It is the third degree manifestation of the Initial Creative Force.
"The Initial Creative Force is but an energy which can bring into being, Original Potential.
"The second degree Creative Force is that energy which binds together this potential—bringing manifestation.
"The third degree Creative Force is that energy known as LOVE.
"Freedom from hate can only be brought into active manifestation by its exact opposite polarity. LOVE is the exact opposite from hate, when in basic manifestation.
"Yet it is more than this—much more.
"Being as it is, an energy which has different octaves of exis-

tence, it is mutable and transmutable upon all of these levels back to its one basic source—thus it is the great energy of the Cosmos.

"Freedom from hate can only be brought into being by the manifestation of LOVE upon all levels of existence.

"LOVE is a natural energy, all pervasive, greater than mind, so therefore, it can be contacted and brought into active manifestation by all terrestrials.

"LOVE is the transmuter of war. It is the Creator of Peace.

"LOVE as such is the Healer of disease.

"Manifestation of The Second Freedom will bring to Terra—Freedom from want.

"Freedom from war.

"Freedom from disease.

"Freedom from one's lower self.

"Freedom from hate.

"Freedom from basic emotionalism.

"The manifestation of this one basic Freedom gives, as its prize, all basic Freedoms, with little exception. How is this manifested?

"LOVE is more than a state of mind—it is a state of whole being.

"When terrestrial man begins to realize his true position in the Cosmos, he must then begin to manifest this great Power.

"LOVE is not the result of ignorance, but the direct result of applied Enlightenment.

"Become Enlightened, gain understanding of the feelings and problems of all peoples and LOVE becomes a living, vibrant, all-pervasive thing.

"In our observations of Terra, we have noted that the slayer of LOVE is hypocrisy. Many, content in their procrastinations, hypocritically talk and bandy this word about, 'til it hath no meaning, save a vague, misunderstood academic one.

"It is an active, living thing.

"The energy—the Freedom called LOVE—does not only exist on your Holy days, but throughout each day and each night.

"If terrestrial man manifests this Power during his waking state, he will also manifest this same Power during his sleep state, when part of the consciousness is still active. As sleep is a state of projection from the physical body brought about by a certain element of consciousness, then the Power—LOVE can still be radiated by this part of consciousness.

"When such things as these are brought into active being throughout your whole lives, then indeed is this great energy released unto all men upon Terra.

"All things living—which means all things upon Terra—respond to the release of this great, all pervasive energy, especially if it be released in its highest form.

"LOVE is not possession. In its highest aspect, it is above all forms of individualization. It is impersonal. It is not binding as is possession, but it brings Freedom.

"Manifest this great, true, impersonal Power in your every thought and action during your waking state, then it will still be manifested by you during your projected state which you call sleep.

"Of all the subjects spoken of in terrestrial Religions, LOVE might have been mentioned more than any other Power; yet, it is the Power which is least understood.

"Know this, for your contemplations; the Chakra in the heart has two faces. The Chakra in the throat has one face. The Chakra in the forehead has three faces. In each and all is the energy called LOVE manifested, but in different degrees. A basic rise of the Power you call Kundalini tends to partially activate one face of the heart Chakra. This often manifests itself as childish emotion; sometimes referred to as sentiment. This is not the LOVE I speak of. The LOVE I speak of radiates from the two faces in balance; from the throat centre; from the centres in the forehead; from all faces in balance. This, terrestrial man, is LOVE.

"LOVE is sacrifice—real sacrifice.

"If ever there was one thing sure, it is this: at your command there is a whole Macrocosmic System filled with this energy. You will be asked, after the Initiation called death, either why you did not use this Power more fully, or why you tended to misuse the basic aspects of it.

"Be prepared for this question, for as sure as God it will be asked —and you will answer.

"Dependent upon that answer, oh my brothers, can be your next life!

"The Second Freedom is LOVE—true LOVE.

"Manifest this—and mould your future.

"All Transmissions now discontinued."

Delivered on Sunday, February 19th, 1961.

LOVE

"Know that, during The Second Freedom, much Power will be released to all world. Many here will be used as channels for this Power, relax, let Power flow through you out to world."

Such instruction as this is nothing new to those people who have been performing the mystic practice of "The Twelve Blessings" (Note 1). But for those who may not have done so, a word of explanation is warranted. The student should, when allowing Spiritual Power to flow through him out to the world, try to be as relaxed and peaceful within himself as possible. Any tension not only impairs the flow of psychic forces activated by Prayers for the world, but also tends to build up more severe tension within the mind and body of the student, who is performing such a practice.

"No need even to guide it, for it will be manipulated by Higher Forces."

The Higher Forces referred to in the text are the Devas. These intelligences live on different planes of existence, which are exactly dovetailed into the planes occupied by terrestrial man. The main function of the Devic Kingdom is the manipulation of all forces, which are necessary to and have bearing upon, the balance of nature. The great tides of mental and psychic energies, which are constantly being conditioned by their passage through the minds of the human race, are also manipulated by the Devas. It is not the work of the Devas to change, either for better or worse, the energies radiated by man. They are only concerned with the direction of such energy fields within the all-pervasive Law of action and reaction. When a stream of mento-psychic energy, which has been grossly distorted by man's wrong thought pattern, is radiated on to the subtle planes, the Devas are bound, by Law, to manipulate this discoloured energy, which causes an unpleasant reaction throughout all nature. Famine, droughts, floods, cyclones and earthquakes are all direct reactions produced through the Devic manipulation of distorted mento-psychic energies emanating from man. On the other hand perfect weather, abundance, freedom from storms and violent earthquakes are the reactions produced when man continually radiates pure Spiritual energies on to the Devic planes.

All serious students should keep these important facts always before them throughout their daily lives, as well as during their future Metaphysical practices (Note 2).

If you choose a correctly balanced practice, such as "The Twelve Blessings"—and it is one of the most potent—in order to send out vibrant Spiritual Power to the world as a whole, then while you are performing such a practice, relax, visualize a pure white Light leaving the heart centre, detach yourself from the result and let the Higher Forces, or the Devic Kingdom, manipulate this Primary Energy on your behalf. Indeed, that is what Saint Goo-Ling advised the attenders to The Second Freedom to do (See Note 1).

"The Second Freedom will be—LOVE.

"Upon Terra this word is wrongly used. LOVE is not the measure of emotion, whether soft or violent, it is something deeper, something greater, something which cannot be measured even in mind conception."

One of the most misunderstood and wrongly used words on this Earth is the word—Love.

All people are capable of expressing true Love, but only a few do so. The word Love, in the average man's dictionary, means something very different from what it really is. Love is pure, uncontaminated energy which is above like or dislike, above possession and certainly above emotion. In fact, the text states exactly what it is.

"LOVE is an all permeating energy which is above mind. It is the third degree manifestation of the Initial Creative Force."

In the beginning there was only potential. Then for some reason known only to The Absolute Itself, this original potential was brought into and bound within manifestation. The forces used to bring this about could only be referred to as Divine Will, Divine Mind, Motion and Sound.

All that we can see, all that we can ever know about, was brought into being within this framework of pure Divine Law. The Absolute saw fit to:

1) Create the original potential, and
2) Introduce those forces into this potential which were designed to bring it into manifestation.

After taking these first two steps, The Absolute then took the third step which resulted in a preservation of manifestation. The great energy of Preservation is known as Love. From this explanation it can be seen that the energy called Love, referred to in the text, is of a very much higher quality than that known to terrestrial man.

"LOVE is the exact opposite from hate, when in basic manifestation."

Love has many octaves of manifestation, the basic octave of which is the exact opposite from hate. In its higher octave of existence—Love is the third degree Creative Force, or Force of Preservation which, because of its very nature, is one of the Primary Forces of continuing Creation.

"Yet it is more than this—much more. Being as it is an energy which has different octaves of existence, it is mutable and transmutable upon all these levels, back to its one basic source—thus it is the great energy of the Cosmos.

"LOVE is a natural energy, all-pervasive, greater than mind, so therefore, it can be contacted and brought into active manifestation by all terrestrials."

The most powerful energies are the natural ones, all of which can be brought into active manifestation, or under control, by each and every one of us, when we choose to do so. We can reach deep within ourselves, find the channels for the flow of this powerful, natural energy of Love and then release it to all mankind. By the all-pervasive Law of Karma which states: "Action and reaction are opposite and equal," we must receive back from mankind the same quality of Love that we radiate. The radiation of pure Love will result in the reception of pure Love. If we radiate these Powers of transmutation, we ourselves are changed for the better. For Love is the energy which transmutes, or raises the vibrations of, all the basic life forces.

"LOVE is the transmuter of war. It is the Creator of Peace. LOVE, as such, is the Healer of disease."

There is no doubt about it being the Healer of disease. Throughout the centuries healings, which some people have described as miracles, have been brought about through the correct use of Prayer.

Now, what is Prayer? Prayer is a way to transmit energy from point A—the prayer, to point B—the person who needs that Prayer. The Prayer energy is carried safely to its destination by the Power of Love.

The Spiritual energy which is sent from the prayer to the recipient was referred to by the Ancient Yogis as, "Prana" or "The Universal Life Force." But, the carrier of that energy is Love. Please note: the energy called pure Love, not the feeling, the emotion, the like or dislike erroneously referred to as—Love (Note 3).

Love itself is a pure energy and as such it is a Healer of disease. How else can you heal dis-ease but by giving—ease. What is disease? Disease is disharmony. How can you transmute disharmony except through the introduction of harmony. So Love is the great harmonizer of the Solar System. It is an active, practical Metaphysical energy; it is not a theoretical or abstract one, neither is it only a feeling.

"Manifestation of The Second Freedom will bring to Terra— Freedom from want. Freedom from war. Freedom from disease. Freedom from one's lower self. Freedom from hate and Freedom from basic emotionalism. The manifestation of this one basic Freedom gives, as its prize, all basic Freedoms with little exception."

These statements show why it is absolutely essential for all Metaphysical students to manifest and continually radiate pure Love. How is this manifested? Through personal purification, through understanding but even more important than these, through the continual Soul inspired charity of selfless Service to others.

"When terrestrial man begins to realize his true position in the Cosmos, he must then begin to manifest this great Power.

"LOVE is not the result of ignorance, but the direct result of applied Enlightenment."

Mankind has to become Enlightened in order to be able to use the mighty energy called Love, correctly. Jesus, Buddha, Patanjali and other great Avatars could use Love correctly, because They were Enlightened Beings. They were Beings, Who believed in action and not theory. They regarded Love, not as an emotion, not only as a state of mind, but as an all-pervasive energy, which They could tune into when They had developed the right state of awareness and radiate outwards again in a very practical manner, to all people. Jesus manipulated this energy in His Healing. He used it as a carrier wave for His enormous magnetic Powers and as a result, He could recall the "dead" and make the lame walk. Man today could also do these things, if he used this potent force correctly.

When mankind becomes Enlightened, when he gains understanding of the feelings and problems of all people, then Love will become a living, vibrant, all-pervasive state of being. He will discover that the more he Loves, the more he is Loved, the more he will be able to Love. So, in this way, man will be able to break himself away from his present vicious circle, that of being ruled by his five basic senses and begin to soar outwards, upwards and onwards towards higher accomplishments.

"In our observations of Terra, we have noted that the slayer of LOVE is hypocrisy. Many, content in their procrastinations, hypocritically talk and bandy this word about, 'till it has no meaning save a vague, misunderstood, academic one.
"It is an active, living thing."
In Metaphysical circles, people should be more than careful how they use the term Love and indeed how they use the Power, which they call Love. In many cases it is not Love which is expressed, but only emotionalism, governed by like and dislike which later deteriorates into basic, animalistic possession.

This is not Love at all. One can Love the world without liking it. One can Love the world without wanting to possess one Soul or body within it.

This is the expression of pure Love.

One has to be extremely careful how this Love energy is used, because of its tremendous Power. It is the only energy which can reproduce itself from itself. For instance, if a stream of Love energy is sent towards an objective and a barrier is put up against it, it will multiply its potency by four and return to the target, until it is received. If you warp the use of this Power and send it, for instance, towards a politician whose policy you are not in agreement with and whose mind you want to change, it will, when it is rejected, multiply itself by four and continue this multiplication while it remains in mental manifestation, until it has some very definite effect upon the politician. This is black magic and not the pure White Magic of radiating true, impersonalized Love energy (Note 4).

"LOVE is not possession."
It should never be used as an excuse for possession. It is the energy we should use to heal, to raise up, to bless. Should it be used wrongly

to give a higher position in the world, then the very nature behind the thought will cause such an involution of the initial thought pattern as to replace the Love energy with base avarice and greed. Sooner or later the Law of Karma will take its toll of all who are guilty of such an involved use of this wonderful Power.

"If terrestrial man manifests this Power during his waking state, he will also manifest the same Power during his sleep state, when part of the consciousness is still active. As sleep is a state of projection from the physical body brought about by a certain element of consciousness, then the Power—LOVE, can still be radiated by this part of consciousness."

Few people know what sleep is. Few realize that sleep is virtually a state of projection, when part of the mind leaves the physical body to perform, either other necessary tasks upon different planes of consciousness or just to wander aimlessly through the lower planes. Man is responsible for his thought and action for 24 hours a day; not only during his waking hours, but during his sleep state as well. If we manifest Love energy in our waking state, then we gradually learn to, automatically, continue this manifestation during our sleep state as well. When we do this, we send out and receive twice the energy we would normally, the Law being exact in this respect: action and reaction being as they are, exactly opposite and equal. This makes it even more important to manifest the great Power of Love throughout every thought and action.

"All things living—which means all things upon Terra—respond to the release of this great, all-pervasive energy, especially if it be released in its highest form."

All things upon Earth which are living, react to Love. Some people are very successful with machinery, because they understand and Love it. No one can hate machinery and still use it successfully. Even so-called "inanimate things" react to this all-pervasive Power. We should try to Love all things, as well as other humans. We should try to even Love the bricks that our house is made of. If we do, a wonderful atmosphere will pervade the house, because the bricks have feeling, they have mind, they are not dead, insensible things; they react to the great Love vibration.

The next time you walk alone in the woods and if you have not done so recently, then soon do so, send out your Love to the grass beneath your feet, to the birds and the trees, to the little animals, to the gnomes and the fairies, which are present even though invisible to you. After you have done this, just stand still, relax and see what happens. You will feel the whole of nature respond to this Power in a very definite manner. You will physically feel vibrations coursing throughout your nervous system, unless you are totally insensible. You will feel as though you have been uplifted, as though you have received a Blessing from somewhere. Try this Spiritual practice and the almost instantaneous, unmistakable response you will receive, should prove to you, beyond all doubt, that all nature reacts to the all-pervasive, Divine Power called—Love.

"In its highest form, it is above all forms of individualization. It is impersonal. It is not binding as is possession, but it brings Freedom."

If a man really and truly Loves the whole world, he really and truly Loves all things equally. He does not just Love a very small part of the world and hate the rest. If you Love all things with an equal intensity, you must experience Freedom. Limitation is brought about, by either being possessed by someone, or by possessing someone or something. If you Love equally, then all things are yours and you are part of all things. As a result you must know a greater Freedom than you do now. This is basic Metaphysical and even physical logic.

"Of all the subjects spoken of in terrestrial Religions, LOVE might have been mentioned more than any other Power, yet, it is the Power which is least understood."

This is true. Some people regard Love as a sweet, suave, almost sickly type of emotionalism. It is not like that. The Yogi, who is detached from man, detached from personality, detached from the world, will manifest a greater Love to a personality and to the world, than the person who is always talking about Love in a very sticky manner, the very nature of which proves that he does not understand this to be the great impersonal Power, which it is.

"Know this, for your contemplations: the Chakra in the heart has two faces. The Chakra in the throat has one face. The Chakra in the forehead has three faces. In each and all is the energy called LOVE manifested, but in different degrees. A basic rise of the Power you

call Kundalini tends to partially activate one face of the Heart Chakra. This often manifests itself as childish emotion; sometimes referred to as sentiment. This is not the LOVE I speak of. The LOVE I speak of radiates from the two faces in balance; from the throat centre; from the centres in the forehead; from all faces in balance."

At the base of the spine there is a very minute atom cluster, the nucleus of which contains the semi-dormant Power, which the Ancients referred to as Kundalini, or the Serpent Power (See Plate 1). Mankind has, through the centuries, been trying to gain the secret of raising and controlling this colossal Power. IN FACT, THE MAIN LESSON THAT MAN HAS TO LEARN UPON EARTH IS THE RISE AND STRICT CONTROL OF KUNDALINI.

Now, the spine is rather like an atom-splitting machine. When natural forces are sent down through the spinal column at a great velocity, they bombard the atoms of Kundalini lodged at the base of the spine and the resultant collision eventually causes a release of Power in its entirety. Then this tremendous primeval force rises through the very narrow channel in the middle of the spine and as it passes through each psychic centre in turn, that centre blossoms out somewhat like a huge brilliant flower. As the Kundalini rises further up the spine, it draws all the energies from the lower psychic centre and takes them up, with it, to the next higher psychic centre, which in turn blossoms out into another great vortex of energy. Again the vortex is slowly and gently closed as the Kundalini is raised even higher up the spine. When a man can control this rise and fall of Kundalini in the spine consciously, then he is on the verge of advanced Initiation (Note 5). When a full rise of Kundalini is brought about, the two centres constituting the heart Chakra are in complete balance and harmony one with another. The throat Chakra is in complete balance and the three centres in the forehead are in complete balance and harmony one with another. When the Adept is capable of this conscious manipulation, within himself, he is then capable of the understanding and use of the impersonal, yet magnificently warm, preservative energy—called Love.

"If ever there was one thing sure, it is this: at your command there is a whole Macrocosmic System filled with this energy. You will be asked after the Initiation called death, either why you did not use this Power more fully, or why you tended to misuse the

basic aspects of it. Be prepared for this question, for as sure as God it will be asked—and you will answer.

Again, Mars Sector 6, in His deep compassion for mankind, is going out of His way to appeal to all to take careful notice of this text, to understand the Divine Energy—Love and He is also impressing upon everyone how vitally important it is to use this energy correctly and frequently.

He is reminding you that, even if you have not thought of this before, it is not too late to start now—at this very moment. The text states quite categorically that you will be asked after death: "Why you did not use this energy correctly," and you will answer this question, when you stand in the Hall of self judgment. Your Higher Self will know why the lower aspects, if you like to put it that way, did not use Love properly.

"Dependent upon that answer, oh my brothers, can be your next life!"

The all-pervasive, perfectly just Law of Karma will impose the limitations necessary upon the next life of everyone, who has not used the Divine Power of Love correctly, not as a punishment, but as an essential teaching. NO ONE CAN ESCAPE THE INEVITABLE EXAMINATION AFTER DEATH AND THE NEXT LIFE OF EVERYONE WILL BE DEPENDENT UPON THE RESULTS OF THIS EXAMINATION. This is a definite statement of Truth and even if some do not like it, it remains just as true—just as inevitable.

"The Second Freedom is LOVE—true LOVE.
"Manifest this—and mould your future!"

In this brilliant summing up, the Master gives, to all students, essential advice which, if taken and strictly acted upon, will save much future misery and involution—will allow you all, to soar onwards and upwards through the gates of Joyous Freedom.

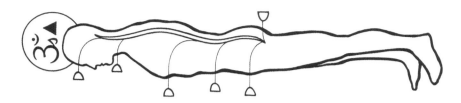

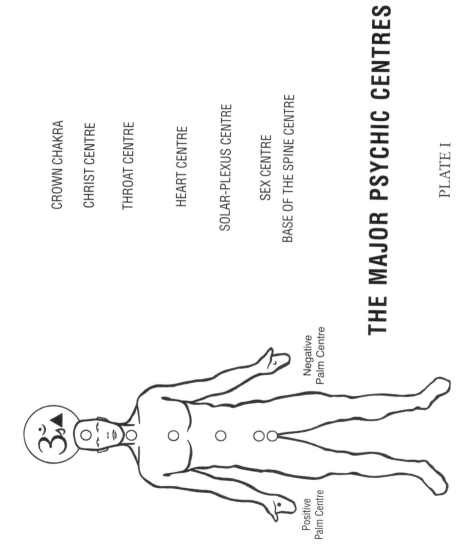

CROWN CHAKRA

CHRIST CENTRE

THROAT CENTRE

HEART CENTRE

SOLAR-PLEXUS CENTRE

SEX CENTRE

BASE OF THE SPINE CENTRE

Negative Palm Centre

Positive Palm Centre

THE MAJOR PSYCHIC CENTRES

PLATE I

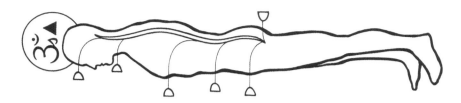

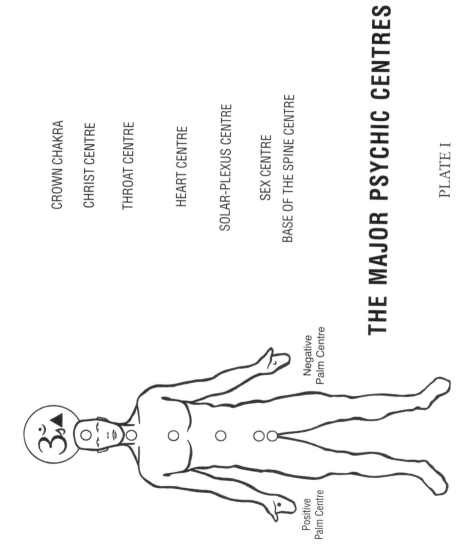

47

AUTHOR'S RECOMMENDATIONS

NOTE 1. *The Twelve Blessings* is a book of mystic Practices as delivered by the Master Jesus through the same author. This book presents an extension of the teachings which Jesus started when on Earth. See also the amazing articles, "Jesus Comes Again" and "Jesus Blesses His Bible," both in *Cosmic Voice* Issue No. 20 (pages 2-20).

NOTE 2. Read the Metaphysical lesson called, *The Devic Kingdom,* for further information.

NOTE 3. Study of the very well-known Metaphysical lesson, *Dynamic Prayer Brings Results,* will teach students how to administer successful Divine Healing through Prayer. See also the Conclusion of *The Nine Freedoms.*

NOTE 4. A very careful study of the Metaphysical lesson, *The Three Forms Of Magic,* is considered absolutely essential for all students, whether advanced or beginners.

NOTE 5. Study the two Metaphysical lessons, *Concentration-Contemplation-Meditation,* and, *The Significance And Development Of The Psychic Centres.* These specially prepared lessons will give the student further information regarding the existence and function of Kundalini. See also Chapters 3 and 5 of *The Nine Freedoms.*

All these recommended books and lessons are obtainable from the publishers of *The Nine Freedoms.*

CHAPTER 3

THE THIRD FREEDOM WILL BE SERVICE

SAINT GOO-LING

A bowl of Prasad, consisting of pieces of sweet cake was placed on the table so that Saint Goo-Ling could bestow His Blessings upon it.

"By Power vested in Me, I Bless this Prasad and sacrifice to Brahma.

"Afterwards each one take Prasad and eat all of it in sacrifice to Brahma. It is Blessed and Holy.

"Throughout the rest of this Operation, same ceremony will be performed.

"Today, again, some who come will be used as channels for energy which will be sent to all world. Also, those who come in physical bodies will be used as channels likewise. In this way, Power will be sent to all who are ready.

"Be open. Let Power flow. Be still. Do not restrict.

"I go."

MARS SECTOR 6

"This is Mars Sector 6 from Satellite No. 3, now in orbit—Neptune.

"The Third Freedom will be—SERVICE.

"Freedom from selfishness is—SERVICE.

"In these days there is much SERVICE which is vitally important to Terra. There are few servers.

"SERVICE is a culmination of experiences which denote the server as being on the ladder of Evolution, firmly on this ladder.

"Those who have a yearning desire to serve and indeed are doing so, are those who have slain selfishness; are those who are gradually overcoming their lower materialistic aspects; are those who are, sometimes slowly, but nevertheless surely, advancing towards Enlightenment.

"In these days upon Terra, it is selfless action, called SERVICE which will count in your Initiations of tomorrow. Your SERVICE to others will be known and you will judge yourselves accordingly.

"If you would burn up your lower Karmic aspects, you would serve.

"If you would, at this very moment, begin to build tomorrow's temple upon the sure foundations of today's right action, you would serve.

"If you would be free from the materialistic prison cunningly devised to enslave you, you would serve.

"If you would be detached from your own petty worries, you would serve.

"If you would enjoy better health, you would serve.

"If you would prepare yourselves for the New World, you would serve.

"SERVICE is indeed a glorious undertaking! It is lasting, for every act of SERVICE is written in everlasting letters of fire in the Akashic Book. When you walk into the Halls of self judgment, you will read what your own hand hath written upon these pages and by the immutable Law of Karma, you will accordingly set limitation upon your rebirth.

"Break away from your own troubles by concentrating upon the sufferings of others.

"Serve in the great Spiritual battle and you can walk with head high and stand in any Hall unafraid to read what be written there.

"The greatest Yoga is—SERVICE.

"The greatest Religion is—SERVICE.

"The greatest act is that act done in—SERVICE.

"Kill possession. Transmute selfishness into SERVICE for others and your reward will come. Enlightenment, like the break of dawn upon the darkest night, will cast the shadows of this night before it.

"Serve—and you will become Enlightened.

"Serve—and you will be practising true selfless Love.

"Serve—and the mighty Power of Kundalini will rise in natural, unforced fashion and open the Chakra jewels in your higher bodies, in will pour inspiration and you will be standing on the verge of the Initiation into Adeptship.

"There are no words great enough to describe the wonder of—SERVICE.

"And no words can describe the crime of selfishness.

"Know this. Whether you like it or not does not matter, it is the Truth. I, Mars, do declare it as such. If you believe it not today, terrestrial man, you will know it in your morrow.

"What is SERVICE but Love in practical action.

"SERVICE is the result of applied Spiritual logic. It is the lasting flower in the garden of Enlightenment. SERVICE is the Jewel in the Rock of Attainment.

"There are many ways to serve upon Terra. Look around you and see—ignorance, suffering, want, hate, greed, selfishness, war, murder, robbery—violence in every form. See how people, the young ones, are being deluded.

"There are many ways, indeed, to serve.

"By your SERVICE you can help to heal those who are sick and you should.

"By your SERVICE you can help to give encouragement and strength to those who are depressed and weak and you should do this.

"By your SERVICE you can throw a dazzling beam of scintillating white vibrant energy into the darkness of a suffering world—and raise it.

"It is—by God it is—the Jewel in the Rock of Attainment.

"It is the great practice in these days.

"One person who is rendering true Spiritual SERVICE, not self delusion, but true Spiritual SERVICE to those who need it, is worth ten who retreat from the suffering of others in order to bring about a state of joy and peace within themselves.

"This declaration do I throw into every mental realm. I would inform those aspirants, who, in total disregard of human needs, retreat into the wilderness: 'Come you hence, for you are fools!'

"SERVICE, my friends is greatness.

"Serve and be great! Nay—be Everlasting.

"All Transmissions now discontinued."

Delivered on Wednesday, February 22nd, 1961.

SERVICE

In the introduction of The Third Freedom, Saint Goo-Ling was passed a bowl of Prasad, which consisted of very carefully made sweet cake. After He had Blessed it, through the author, He gave to everyone a great mystic secret by saying: *"I Bless this Prasad and sacrifice to Brahma."*

If all men were to sacrifice all they ate to God, they would be strictly obeying a very deep and significant occult Law. The body is a vehicle in which the Soul gains experience in materialism. The very act of sacrificing food, or fuel, for this vehicle, to Brahma or God, as you might call It, is a very significant one in as much as you are virtually sacrificing this food, so that the Soul may gain experience and thus progress through Evolution. So that the Soul may, eventually, when it has gained control over all physical matter, be bathed in the Light of the Pure Spirit.

Of course, once food is Blessed by a Master, that food becomes Holy. Once food has been sacrificed to God, that food becomes Sacred and every morsel of it must be eaten. It would not be wise for anyone to sacrifice food in Service to God unless he intended to eat every morsel, because he would break the Law. Anything which is Blessed is so Holy that it must be treated as Sacred. With this outlook, food takes on a very different importance than it did before. No longer do we eat because we like the taste of food, no longer do we pander to our most basic animal-like instincts. We eat because an intake of fuel is necessary to keep the body alive, so that it may gain a fuller experience, so that it might be a point where the negative and positive poles of consciousness intersect and self-consciousness is manifested. So that, eventually, this point of consciousness might nourish the Super-Conscious essence, so that it might be flooded by the Light of Pure Spirit, which only occurs in the true Meditative state.

"Today, again, some who come will be used as channels for energy which will be sent out to all world. Also, those who come in physical bodies will be used as channels likewise."

There is an inference in this statement by Saint Goo-Ling which has deep occult significance. By it, He obviously meant that not only were The Nine Freedoms attended by people in Earth physical bodies, but also by lifestreams in etheric bodies. Indeed, such intelligences outnumbered the physical attenders, several thousands of times.

In order to understand how this was possible, a few words of explanation about the other planes of existence are deemed necessary. It must be remembered that death is an Initiation (Note 1). It is a time when the intelligence passes from the lower room—this Earth, into the upper classroom—one of the other planes of existence. Now, these planes of existence are formed out of a physical matter which is very much more subtle and tenuous than the physical matter we know on Earth. In fact, so tenuous is the material out of which these planes are formed, that they exactly dovetail into the physical plane of Earth without anyone becoming aware of it, unless they have had years of rigorous training in the psychic science of clairvoyance (Note 2). Therefore, after death, the intelligence leaves the physical body with the same characteristics, yearnings and hopes it possessed while on this Earth and it goes to another plane of existence in order to pass through other experiences necessary for Evolutionary progress.

If a terrestrial acquires a great interest in the higher occult Truths, that interest lives with him when he passes from the Earth plane to the other, more subtle physical planes of existence.

It is a known fact that, whenever any Metaphysical operation is undertaken on Earth, a "light" is also ignited on the subtle realms. An entity who had the yearning for such a "light" would be attracted to it. In the case of The Nine Freedoms, thousands of discarnate entities, who inhabited the subtle realms while awaiting their reincarnation on Earth, actually did attend. Hence the inference by Saint Goo-Ling that some of these would be used for the Power Manipulation which was carried on during the time The Nine Freedoms was given.

There is a very important point which should be stressed here and it is this: according to the ancient mystic "Upanishads" the greatest gift that one man can give to another is—Wisdom (Note 3). As this is so, then the greatest crime that a man can commit is to give that which is not wise, or cause confusion in the minds of people by giving them the wrong teachings. The right teachings, which are true according to the known Laws, not only help the people now living upon this Earth in their journey through Evolution, but also help those discarnate entities who are awaiting their rebirth on to the Earth plane. At the opposite end of the scale, confusing, incorrect teachings, not only hold back the searching student of Truth upon this Earth, but also delay the Evolution of the discarnate entities as well. Because a teacher is held to be completely responsible for his teachings under Karmic Law, his Karma, conditioned by causing untrue and confusing teachings to be broadcast, would be doubly marked against him.

This vitally important aspect of the Law should be given the priority of consideration it undoubtedly deserves by everyone upon the teaching platforms of the world. Of course the few genuine and qualified Metaphysical teachers do know of this Law and strictly adhere to it. However it is a pitiful shame, that so much confusion is being spread, both upon the Earth plane and throughout the more basic psychic realms, by "speakers" who have not even begun to study their subjects correctly, never mind practise them!

Scores of people, in misery and grief caused by wrong and conflicting occult and religious "teachings" have sought the advice of The Aetherius Society. Fortunately, it was possible to give the right help to every student who was genuinely searching for Truth. Sometimes such a Spiritual renaissance was caused that it meant a whole new, brighter outlook and a fuller life to them. When the lasting Truths were explained with patience and perseverance and these were found, by the students themselves, to really work, they were then ready to clear their minds of the falsehoods put there by unknowledgeable, unqualified "speakers" who had previously deceived them.

"The Third Freedom will be—SERVICE.

"Freedom from selfishness is—SERVICE. SERVICE is a culmination of experiences which denote the server as being on the ladder of Evolution, firmly on this ladder."

Hundreds of years ago, the great man was he who cut his association so completely from mankind that he spent his life alone in some wilderness, in order to gain the deeper Meditative states. The same is not true today! The greatest man now, is he who could gain the deep Meditative states and yet surrenders them so that he may serve in a practical manner among mankind.

There is no doubt that civilization is tottering on the brink of its own destruction. If, even a small portion of this civilization is to be saved, then it is Service which will save it. In the text, Mars Sector 6 states quite categorically that the server has proved the fact that he is firmly planted on the ladder of Evolution. In other words, one cannot be evolving unless one is serving; there is no doubt about this.

Whether the world likes it or believes it or not, this is the Truth and it is an unalterable Truth.

"In these days upon Terra, it is selfless action, called SERVICE, which will count in your Initiations of tomorrow. Your SERVICE to others will be known and you will judge yourselves accordingly."

There comes an Initiation called "death" in the existence of every person upon this Earth. During this Initiation, mankind passes from the gross physical body, from the lower room, into the upper room. He still inhabits a physical body although it is made of a different substance than the body he left behind on Earth. He still lives in full consciousness, in full memory on another world and he still learns the lessons of that plane. He is answerable to the great Law of Karma. It depends upon his actions in this present materialistic life as to what level of consciousness he attains on this other realm while he is awaiting rebirth on this Earth.

"Your Initiations of tomorrow," here refers to the Initiation which all men have to undergo in the Hall of self judgment. There, the Super-Consciousness will judge the lower-consciousness and it will choose the exact time for rebirth in another physical body on Earth. It will even choose the place and the parents which are to help bring that body into physical manifestation. It will judge the environment which is necessary so that the lower aspects of the consciousness may learn the lessons necessary in order to evolve. A great deal of suffering can easily be relieved if the Super-Consciousness does not need to impose gross limitations upon the reincarnating consciousness.

The text states that Service will count in these Initiations. If we serve our fellowmen with a completely unselfish motive in this life, we will have advanced so tremendously that, in the next life it will be unnecessary to impose gross limitations upon ourselves. We need not be born blind, deformed or in a community which has its periods of flood and drought, starvation and disease. We need not be born under the cruel heel of a tyrannical dictator, as some lifestreams are, in order to gain certain experiences from such gross and painful limitations. Such conditions could not even exist, never mind be necessary, if mankind made up its mind to serve mankind. We are cells in the body of one great limitless whole. If we hurt another, we hurt ourselves. If we help another, we help ourselves. The Law of Karma has stated this and it cannot ever be revoked, because IT IS GOD (Note 4).

Service is a necessary procedure in these days, not only to help the whole of civilization, but because of a series of actions which must be performed by all of us if we are to gain those experiences which will help us in our lives to come.

"If you would burn up your lower Karmic aspects, you would serve. If you would, at this very moment, begin to build tomorrow's temple upon the sure foundations of today's right action, you would serve."

Man tends to forget that, whether he likes it or not, he is, at least to some extent, his brother's keeper. Instead of living in this knowledge, the majority are completely attached to their own small materialistic world. They are attached to position and often have to fight hard to keep it. They are attached to the discomforts of their own and the bodies of those whom they consider to be their nearest relatives. But there is more in life than these personal attachments.

"If you would be detached from your own petty worries—you would serve. If you would enjoy better health, you would serve."

The author remembers a time when, in the early days, he was studying the art of Spiritual Healing in England. One healer came along to the Healing Temple and he was seen to stagger. The author went to him and made him sit down. Earlier that day, this man had suffered an accident to his knee and he had gashed it very nastily. The author, expressing concern for the wound, stated that he needed healing more than some of his patients.

"Yes, I do, but later," was the healer's reply.

After he had given Healing to a dozen patients, some of them not nearly as ill as himself, he came from the Temple and although mentally tired, his knee had improved a great deal. During the time the healer had been attached to the suffering of others, he had been detached from his own pain. Even as he lent a helping hand to his patients, his own wound became healed.

Two or three days later, the wound in his knee was cured completely and he was as vigorous as ever.

There is no doubt that the more we think of our own petty physical and mental pains, the worse they become. There are many people who have appealed to all kinds of healers for help, who have little wrong with them. Such people should be sent to walk the wards of some of the hospitals of the world, to mix with, help, serve and heal people who are really ill, then they would also be cured.

"Every act of SERVICE is written in everlasting letters of fire in the Akashic Book."

The Akashic Records contain, in minute detail, the complete history of every individual's thought and action. The complete story of all terrestrial events is impressed upon the etheric seas through which Earth makes Her continual passage. So clearly defined are the pictures in the almost infinitely mutable Ether, that the Illumined Ones need only to study the Ethers around any Planet to learn Its complete history. They can also look at the aura of a man and read his history impressed therein. The great hand of Karma writes up the total history of the world in the great Ether belt around the Earth. So also does a man, just as surely, write his own history upon the Akashic Records within his own auric bodies and every mental picturization has its effect for good or bad in this and in future lives.

"When you walk into the Hall of self judgement, you will read what your own hand hath written upon these pages and by the immutable Law of Karma, you will accordingly set limitation upon your rebirth."

The Super-Consciousness will not judge cruelly. It will judge in the way it has to judge by Law and if it deems that necessary experiences can only be gained by limitations, then these will be imposed. We cannot ever break away from the wheel of rebirth, unless we have learned every lesson necessary to us upon this Earth. We must master all of our lower aspects and we must have transmuted them in the fires of complete experience, if we are ever to take our rightful place upon the higher spheres of existence. How can we leave this classroom until we have passed the final examination with the necessary honors? We would be lost on a higher sphere of existence if we could not live on this lower plane correctly. It would be the cruelest thing which could happen to us to be suddenly transported to another, more highly evolved Planet until ready. We would be so completely out of place, so absolutely alone, that we would be in a worse position than a head-hunting pigmy would be in were he suddenly transported to a large city and made to live with the mathematics professor of a university. So therefore, it is necessary for the Super-Consciousness to set limitations upon rebirth, to calculate the exact time and environment of that rebirth, so that a chain of predictable experiences may teach the lessons which are absolutely essential to Spiritual growth.

"The greatest Yoga is—SERVICE. The greatest Religion is—SERVICE. The greatest act is that act done in—SERVICE."

Without this lesson we will remain upon Earth for 10,000 lives if necessary, until eventually we are tempered in the fires of experience, are softened so that we can transmute our basic animalistic selfishness into the great Light of Service and continue to dispense this willingly. No one can escape this. We cannot ever attain Enlightenment unless we serve. We might have great knowledge and yet be selfish. We still have not gained Wisdom. Probably in another life our knowledge will be locked up in our memories and we will have to work for life after life to gain remembrance of it again. Whether it is necessary to do this or not, must depend upon each individual case. One thing is sure, we will never gain true Enlightenment unless we serve.

"Serve—and the mighty Power of Kundalini will rise in natural, unforced fashion and open the Chakra jewels in your higher bodies, in will pour inspiration and you will be standing on the verge of the Initiation into Adeptship."

If you refer to Plate 1, you will see that man has Chakras or psychic centres in different positions throughout his body. Each one of these psychic centres is rather akin to a small flood gate. When the great primeval Power of Kundalini, which resides at the base of the spine, rises up the spine, each of these flood-gates is opened in turn. When this happens, each one is seen to possess many different attributes within it. Each flood-gate or psychic centre takes in through itself some of the aspects of mind. Unthinking man is he who has the psychic centres only barely working. When thinking man begins to move the great Fire of Kundalini, She pierces these centres and gives them tremendous energy, so that they work in a balanced fashion. Such a vortex of Power is created that a magnetic demand is made on outside mind which flows in, as an energy, unimpeded.

When the text states: *"In will pour inspiration"* it means just this. As each psychic centre is opened and controlled, then all the aspects of mind are likewise brought under control, until eventually, when Kundalini is risen high enough in the spine and the higher centres are pierced and blossom like great vortices of magnificent, natural Fire, in will pour the deep aspects of Illumination. We will then go into the elevated states of Meditation. We will be at one with that upon which we Meditate (Note 5).

When we serve others in an unselfish fashion, we are performing the highest Yoga and the greatest Religion. We are gaining control over the great Fire of Kundalini to such an extent that we will not have to force any rise of this Power. It will rise in a natural fashion, little by little, until we will be standing on the verge of the Initiation of Adeptship.

THE MAIN REASON WHY YOU ARE ON EARTH IS TO LEARN TO CONTROL THE MIGHTY POWERS OF KUNDALINI WITHIN YOU.

Service will help to bring to you this most treasured of all mystical jewels.

Indeed are the words of the script correct: *"There are no words great enough to describe the wonder of SERVICE."*

"SERVICE is the result of applied Spiritual Logic. It is the lasting flower in the garden of Enlightenment. SERVICE is the Jewel in the Rock of Attainment."

Service is not the result of ignorance, but the guaranteed and direct result of applied logic. The logical man is the serving man. The ignorant man is the selfish man. The selfish man is he who has not even gained control of his lowest psychic centre. The serving man is the man who has gained some measure of control of even the higher psychic centres and he has applied to his act of Service, a definite type of Spiritual logic, which tells him that he must not be selfish as he is a part of the whole. All his actions refer back to himself and he reaps the reactions from these. So the logical man is the man who will learn and strictly abide by the Law. The ignorant man cares not for the Law and suffers as a result of his unenlightened selfishness.

If ever there were a superb definition of pure charity, a veritable aphorism in the annals of lasting Truth, a philosophical hub around which the wheels of action of all men should revolve, it is the prophetic sentence from the text:

"SERVICE is the Jewel in the Rock of Attainment."

Upon this single realization a new world could easily be built—today!

"There are many ways to serve upon Terra. Look around you and

see—ignorance, suffering, want, hate, greed, selfishness, war, murder, robbery—violence in every form. See how people, the young ones, are being deluded."

This passage needs no explanation; it needs to be remembered—always.

"By your SERVICE you can help to heal those who are sick and you should."

The second largest Religion on Earth today, numerically speaking, was founded by a great Spiritual Healer, Jesus of Nazareth. He was a Being who demonstrated Spiritual Healing whenever He had the opportunity to do so. He founded the Christian Religion on His ability to demonstrate His Powers of Healing. It is the very essence of the Christian Religion. When we are told that we, by our Service, can heal those who are sick and we should do so, it means that indeed it is our responsibility to do so.

You should always remember that every man on Earth can give Spiritual Healing; that it is the birthright of mankind to pass on Divine Healing Power and it is also his duty (Note 6).

"One person who is rendering true Spiritual SERVICE, not self delusion, but true Spiritual SERVICE to those who need it, is worth ten who retreat from the suffering of others in order to bring about a state of joy and peace within themselves."

There are many people who delude themselves into believing that they serve others. There are some people who may think, because they are charitable towards one person who is near and dear to them, that they are giving true Spiritual Service to the world. It is not so. The men and women who are giving Spiritual Service to the world are those who will go out into the by-ways and give Healing, advice and help to complete strangers. The true Spiritual server is he who will charge himself with the great Universal Life Forces and send a stream of magnetic Healing energies to his own enemies! It is not a test of Service to give Healing to those you love. It is a test of true Service to give Healing to those you dislike. This is what the Master means by self delusion. There are many students who believe, because they attend a meeting once a week, or a church of some kind every Sunday and because they say an odd Prayer at that church, that they are giving true Spiritual Service. This is not Spiritual Service. Those people are attending the places they want to attend, not the places where they are most needed! We must be careful not to allow ourselves to be deluded into the erroneous belief that we are serving, when we are not doing so. The true server is he who is willing to suffer in his Service.

"This declaration do I throw into every mental realm. I would inform those aspirants, who, in total disregard of human needs, retreat into the wilderness:'Come you hence, for you are fools!'"

Probably never before has a statement like this been made by a Cosmic Master of the undoubted calibre of Mars Sector 6. It was the vogue, at one time, to retreat into the wilderness, away from mankind and there to gain the lasting states of joy. Mars Sector 6 condemns those as fools who do this. In The Twelve Blessings, the Master Jesus said something similar, namely: "I say unto you, man, he who in total disregard of Universal suffering does search in these days for Peace will find it not. For alas, ye are commanded even now, as ye were yesterday, to spread yourselves in sacrificial action throughout your suffering world." (Extract from *The Twelve Blessings* page 34, given by the Master Jesus through the author on August 31st, 1958, published by The Aetherius Press—England.) (Note 7).

In his struggle for supremacy over his own lower aspects, man needs all the help he can get. We are given the chance to help the whole of humanity and if we do not take this opportunity, but think in a self-centred manner only about our own advancement, we cannot ever gain true Enlightenment. It has been stated that there are two "Buddhas" on this world. One of these, often found in India and Thibet, has detached himself from suffering mankind, to go into the wilderness, away from the restricting vibrations of man, away from the petty squabbles and all those conditions which will hold him back, in order to make his body and mind still so that he can taste the ecstatic joy of certain Illumination. The other "Buddha" is he who can go into the wilderness any time he desires, is he who, even in the middle of a city, if he can spare the time, could sit upon the floor, practise his breathing exercises, his great Mantras and raise the Kundalini above the heart centre, so that he can pass into a deep state of undisturbable peace; so that he can bathe in the lake of this lasting peace, so that his Soul can leap in wondrous joy as it is caressed by the gentle, magic fingers of the All-Knowing Spirit; but yet, will detach himself from reality and attach himself to unreality, not because he wants or likes to do so, but because he feels he has to do so, because he has applied a greater Spiritual Logic than the first type of "Buddha" had ever dreamed of. Such an Adept sees that, while there is one diseased cell in the whole, the whole cannot be complete. He realizes that he is able to help raise the whole and because of that, it is his duty to God to do so. Of the two, the second "Buddha" is by far the greater.

The script says this to us in a definite meaningful manner:

"Serve and be great! Nay—be Everlasting."

No better advice has ever been given than this, for here is a sure workable key to the door of Freedom—to the gate of Cosmic experience.

Oh, would that such a statement could be painted in all colours upon a single terrestrial flag; so that all men could be encouraged to look up to and always act in the Light of this wisdom. Why, in one single year a new Millenium of true Peace could be introduced and firmly established within the hearts of men and throughout all terrestrial life. This is the way. This is the promise—come on, all of you, forward into Service—Enlightenment and—Life!

AUTHOR'S RECOMMENDATIONS

NOTE 1. See "What is Death," in *Cosmic Voice*, Issue No. 21, for a complete Transmission delivered by Mars Sector 6, entirely devoted to an explanation of this Initiation.

NOTE 2. Study *How To Develop Your Clairvoyant Powers*, an enlightening and practical lesson of educational interest to all.

NOTE 3. There are numerous translations of, "The Upanishads," which can be obtained from any good occult book shop. This brilliant philosophical work is recommended to all students as a serious study.

NOTE 4. See *Karma And Reincarnation*, for further enlightenment regarding the Divine Law.

NOTE 5. Study the specially written Metaphysical lessons, *Concentration—Contemplation—Meditation*, and *The Significance And Development Of The Psychic Centres*, for further enlightenment regarding these vital subjects.

NOTE 6. *The Practices of Aetherius*, and *Your Higher Self Through Yoga*, will teach students how to give effective Divine Healing to others in need.

Diligent practice of the mystic exercises given in these two booklets will enable serious occult students to become so filled with the Universal Life Force that they can radiate their enhanced magnetism in a powerful Healing stream to all those who are weak and in need of this uplifting and strengthening Divine Healing Power. A careful study and practice of the Metaphysical techniques fully explained in the lessons, *The Secret Of Dynamic Absent Healing*, and *Dynamic Prayer Brings Results*, will take the student out of the kindergarten of theory into the senior school of practice and into true Service to humanity. See also the Prayers given in the Conclusion of *The Nine Freedoms*.

NOTE 7. *The Twelve Blessings* is a textbook of mystical practices given by the Master Jesus and is highly recommended as a study and practice for students of *The Nine Freedoms*.

All above recommended lessons and books are obtainable from the publishers of *The Nine Freedoms*.

CHAPTER 4

THE FOURTH FREEDOM WILL BE ENLIGHTENMENT

SAINT GOO-LING

"This Prasad is Blessed as symbol of sacrifice to Brahma. Whole Blessed as symbol of sacrifice to Brahma.

"Afterwards dispense Prasad to all; eat as sacrifice to Brahma and all of it.

"Now, today, Fourth Freedom will be given. Again, some of those who come will be used as channels for Power. Also those who come in physical bodies will be used as channels for Power which will be radiated.

"Power radiated during Nine Freedoms will have certain effect upon country of America. This effect will be to stop violent earthquakes which were due at this time; so tune in.

"This does not mean that America is guaranteed free from earthquakes, but does mean that man coming together with right motive can bring about some Divine Intervention.

"I go."

MARS SECTOR 6

"This is Mars Sector 6 reporting from Satellite No. 3, now in Magnetization Orbit—Terra, during Magnetization Period No. 1, present phase.

"The Fourth Freedom will be—ENLIGHTENMENT.

"Freedom from ignorance can be brought about by all terrestrials who are willing to expend sufficient energy to bring this elevated state into being. There is but one major sin upon Terra—that is ignorance.

"Bravery, dispensation of pure Love, Service, these attributes can

64

help the aspirant to bring ENLIGHTENMENT into being.

"ENLIGHTENMENT is a result of the controlled application of specific energies and procedures towards a predetermined end.

"Physical man can predetermine the end of his physical energy and cause this to be used in its best sense according to the Law.

"Mental man can so control his picturization that he can direct his mental energies towards a goal which is in all-wise constructive, a goal of Service, of Spiritual cooperation. A great beam of creative, controlled, mental energy can be directed towards all terrestrials, so that those ready will be mentally transmuted by this constructive, creative beam of energy. Mental man can form those visualizations only which are constructive, which help to bring into being a transmutation of all things up to the Higher Planes.

"Psychic man can escape from his prison of psychic frustration by tasks such as the dispensation of energies upon a psycho-Spiritual level, such as the rendering of Spiritual Healing. Of all tasks capable to psychic man, this is the most beneficial.

"Psychic man can so control the subtle Universal Life Forces that he can bring about strict mental control. By so doing, he is capable of concentration. He can, at this stage, so enhance his concentrative abilities that he is capable of contemplation, with open-minded diligence, which will bring about even greater awareness, a greater understanding and which will begin to open the door of ENLIGHTENMENT.

"The next essential step he can then take is the transmutation of mental energies upon the plane of inspiration, called high Intuition. This is brought about by strict control and the manipulation of the individual's Karmic pattern through Service—and so on.

"At this stage he is then capable of Meditation. Through such Meditation the aspirant opens the door, even wider, so that the brilliant, everlasting vibration of ENLIGHTENMENT may forever surround him.

"These are the essential steps to ENLIGHTENMENT. There is not an easy path. Some passages are shorter, yet more dangerous, than others. This you know.

"The Freedom—ENLIGHTENMENT, is the fruit which can be cultivated in the Spiritual garden of terrestrial man—if he tends it with sufficient care, sufficient kindness, sufficient patience, sufficient tolerance. If he tends it with intelligence; if he tends it by manipulating his Karmic pattern through the right Service, this will grow, blossom and will bear all fruits. Heed ye well, terrestrials.

"These are the ways to your Freedom. These are the signs which mark the stony path. These are the tests which you will be given. Mark them well, follow them well and success will be yours.

"Know this: ENLIGHTENMENT is Freedom from ignorance.

"Ignorance is the result of the complication devised by terrestrial man, therefore, ENLIGHTENMENT is simplicity. Note that. Use that as the text for your contemplation and eventually, when Meditation is possible, much will be revealed.

"Note this also: ENLIGHTENMENT cannot dawn while the clouds of indiscrimination cover the skies of your mentality. Discriminate. You have been told how to do this; do it—and go into ENLIGHTENMENT.

"While you slip, like one of your animals from place to place, chewing here and there, you will not gain ENLIGHTENMENT.

"I have instructed you before, to choose well, then stand fast in order to know God. This you must be prepared to do.

"Note this: I speak of Freedom—not petty freewill. There is a God of difference.

"Serve, manipulate your Karmic pattern, then you will be allowed to walk through the dawn of ENLIGHTENMENT.

"All Transmissions now discontinued."

Delivered on Sunday, February 26th, 1961

THE KARMIC SCALES

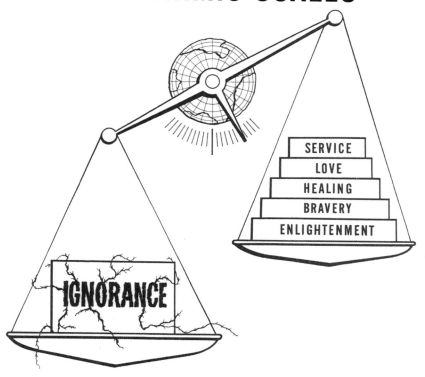

SERVICE
LOVE
HEALING
BRAVERY
ENLIGHTENMENT

IGNORANCE

PLATE 2

The illustration shows, in an easily understandable manner, the state of world Karma today. Such a Karmic pattern, moulded by all terrestrial thought and action, does not allow the Solar Hierarchy to use energy on behalf of mankind unless considerable effort is first expended by man. Delivery of The Nine Freedoms constituted an action which was tantamount to a Divine Intervention on behalf of mankind. Not only were Truths of the greatest value expressed for the first time, but also at least one major catastrophic earthquake was held up for a considerable time, to say the least (see next page). This constitutes a living PROOF of the authenticity of the Source of the mystic text and also proves that the sincere effort, suffering and Prayer of the few were answered by the Great Ones who gave this protection to the unthinking masses.

ENLIGHTENMENT

It was during the introduction to The Fourth Freedom that Saint Goo-Ling intimated, for the first time, the reason for the Powers radiated in coincidence with the delivery of the mystical text.

"Power radiated during Nine Freedoms will have certain effect upon country of America. This effect will be to stop violent earthquakes which were due at this time; so tune in."

A dramatic confirmation and well authenticated proof of the validity of this statement came almost a month LATER in the English newspaper *The Daily Express*, Monday, March 20th, 1961. According to a timely, well-written article, one of the leading earthquake scientists in the world, whose current research includes the Californian fault lines, stated that he could not realize or fully understand, why an earthquake had not already devastated Los Angeles. Indeed was great Power radiated through the Mental Channel who was used to give these great Teachings to the world, as well as through the people who attended and those who cooperated in other countries so that they could be used as human channels for this Power.

"This is Mars Sector 6, reporting from Satellite No. 3, now in Magnetization Orbit—Terra, during Magnetization Period No. 1, present phase."

See the end of this chapter for illustrations and further information regarding Satellite No. 3. Also study, "The Glory of Ascension," at the end of Chapter 6 for an eye-witness description of the inside of this immense Space Station.

"The Fourth Freedom will be—ENLIGHTENMENT.
"Freedom from ignorance can be brought about by all terrestrials who are willing to expend sufficient energy to bring this elevated state into being. There is but one major sin upon Terra—that is ignorance."

There is no doubt that the more you analyze this statement, the more Truth it is seen to contain. War and crime are a result of ignorance. The way we live our present life is, to the greatest extent, the result of ignorance, which is the one and only sin. If "satan" could have another name, then surely it must be "ignorance." The opposite of ignorance is—Enlightenment.

"ENLIGHTENMENT is a result of the controlled application of specific energies and procedures towards a predetermined end."

There are three main ways in which man takes usable energy into his body. In order of importance these are breathing, drinking and eating. But, man should not only breathe, drink and eat; the animals do that. He is above the animals inasmuch as, unlike the more basic life-forms, he possesses self-consciousness. This self-consciousness brings with it a greater responsibility than the basic consciousness of the animal. Because of this, man is completely responsible for the controlled use of all the Universal Life Force upon every breath he breathes. It is his duty, according to the Divine Law, to use the Pranic energies contained in the liquid he drinks and the food he eats, in a way which will most benefit his brothers. It is the duty of man to Spiritualize all mass. When he does so, then there is no doubt that such a controlled use of energy towards a predetermined end will bring that end into being. If that end has been predetermined as—Enlightenment, then he can logically enjoy this elevated state (Note 1).

"Physical man can predetermine the end of his physical energy and cause this to be used in its best sense according to the Law."

We can all use our bodies in such a way as to be either creative or destructive machines. If we destroy, then we will be destroyed. If we use our physical strength to build up, we will, as a direct reaction from this, be given even a greater strength to enable us to become even more creative so that all of our undertakings may become essentially useful to all men.

"Mental man can so control his picturization that he can direct his mental energies towards a goal which is in all-wise constructive, a goal of Service, of Spiritual cooperation."

As we are responsible for the way we use our physical bodies, we are also directly responsible for the way we use our mental picturizations. If we send out a thought form of hate towards another person, that destructive thought form does the other great damage, even though this may not be apparent at the time. The thought form is made of "mind-stuff" which will react upon another's auric envelope. This reaction will later have a further reaction upon the mental and physical man within that aura. So, a thought of hate will cause the man it is sent against, some definite physical and mental damage. If, on the other hand, our picturization is so controlled as to be all-wise constructive and we direct this transmuting beam of energy towards another, he will receive upliftment and assistance from this action. Again the reaction may not be apparent at the time, but sooner or later it must, after its reaction upon the aura of the other, react upon the mental and physical being living within that aura and it must help him in some way or other. This is the occult Law around which all things evolve. We must all realize that thoughts are living forms. Because we cannot see a thought, does not mean to say that, once it is thought, it is immediately taken out of manifestation. When we create a thought form, it is put into manifestation and it remains there until we consciously take it from manifestation; until we absorb that mental form back into ourselves and transmute it on to a higher energy plane. One of the lessons that self-consciousness must teach is that, thought can be created and once created—it lives. It has a very definite form and performs a directed function. If it is a Healing thought, then it has a particular shape and many different colours and it will remain in manifestation until it is transmuted and used by the person to whom we direct that Healing thought form (Note 2).

Every action begins with a thought. Some people believe that if they so hate another that they would like to strike him, but do not allow themselves to do so but yet propel their hate thought form towards the other, they have displayed good control. This is not true. They have merely controlled the least powerful aspect of their being, which is the physical. Much more powerful is the mental aspect of man. Because a man might have controlled a physical arm so that it did not move and hit the other, does not exonerate him from the Karma of sending out the thought form of hate towards the aura of the other; a thought form which will, like a rapier, pierce the aura of the other to such an extent that, sooner or later, it will do some damage. In order to gain Enlightenment, everyone must not only control physical action, but control all mental actions as well. It must be remembered, once and for all, that a thought is just as much an action as a physical deed is. The great man is he who controls his thought and thereby controls his action, so that all of his expenditure of energy is in every way constructive.

"Psychic man can escape from his prison of psychic frustration by tasks such as the dispensation of psychic energies upon a psy-

cho-Spiritual level, such as the rendering of Spiritual Healing. Of all tasks capable to psychic man, this is the most beneficial."

There is no doubt in these days of so-called civilization, that many people suffer from frustrations of one kind or another. Mental frustration seems to be the order of man's daily suffering. But psychic frustration is even worse than this for it causes a blockage in the subtle nervous system which will manifest later in the mental and physical bodies as some kind of disease. In this case a psycho-somatic condition will develop, later to cause a reflection of itself upon the physical body. If someone, who has, in the past, carefully and methodically developed and used his psychic powers, stops using them, he will suffer very acutely from psychic frustration. If, for instance, you are used to praying and radiating your Power often to suffering mankind, then you stop suddenly, without replacing the practice with a similar constructive exercise, you will begin to discover that you have a severe tension building up within the mental and physical structure. If you allow this condition to continue, it will manifest itself in many ways. One very detrimental way in which this psychic frustration may manifest is the leaning towards an overindulgence in the sex practice which is dangerous, unless very strictly controlled. In this way you will tend to, not only sap your mental or physical strength, but also divert the stream of psychic energies from an upwards flow towards the higher centres, to a downwards flow towards the sex centre, with a resultant further dissipation of energy. Further sexual participation will bring some apparent relief to the psycho-somatic condition of such frustration, but this relief will only be of a very temporary nature. The psychic energies will again build up in the subtle, or as the Yogis call it, the "nadic" nervous system. Again they will either have to be wasted or made to rise upwards, such as they do in Prayer or Spiritual Healing, for instance, or they will tend to come downwards, putting tremendous pressure on the sex centre and the glands in that region thereby producing an animalistic sexual yearning which can lead to even further dissipation of the vital life energy, leaving as a result of this a fake, unlasting relief from tension. If mankind allows this condition to continue, he not only dissipates his psychic powers, but most surely will keep the Power of Kundalini down to such an extent that it will only operate through the sex centre and gradually, the higher Chakras, being starved of vitalizing energy, will become ossified. The whole aura will become so dense in one thus afflicted, that he will no longer be open to the subtle stimulation of advanced mind, neither will he be open to the Intuitive forces which can only enter through the higher centres and which can be translated and understood only by a highly sensitized, fully aware brain mechanism. Over-indulgence in sex is like taking an extremely powerful drug. Man takes a drug in order to relieve certain conditions but this drug has a side effect, which brings on other conditions, causing other yearnings. He takes more of the drug in order to quench these developed thirsts which have arisen within his body. More potent side effects are produced. If he continues, such a person becomes an addict to the drug especially if it is one of the opiates. To take a drug in its right place, under strict medical control, is something very different from this. To indulge in the practice of sex under very strict mental control, in order to propagate the race only, is very different from the animal-like indulgence in sex in order to produce a false relief from the yearning caused by psychic frustration. The text states that tasks, such as the dispensation of psychic energies upon the psycho-Spiritual level, such as Spiritual Healing, are not only very beneficial to the suffering recipient, but will relieve the psychic frustrations felt by the more sensitive people in these days (Note 3).

"Psychic man can so control his subtle Universal Life Forces that he can bring about strict mental control. By so doing, he is capable of concentration."

Now, before we can appreciate this, we must ask: what is concentration? (Note 4.)

Concentration is the result of controlled thought, directed towards a predetermined end. If we sit down with the idea of concentrating on the words of this text, we should concentrate on them to the exclusion of all else. If, while studying, we suddenly remember an incident which occurred yesterday, our mind leaps quickly over to the memory of the happening, draws certain conclusions from it and returns to the text again. The mind does not concentrate on both things at once, but tends to move from one objective to the other. Wherever it is directed by the lesser will, so it will concentrate. It is just as easy to concentrate on this text as it is on the colour of a beautiful picture, or on a pain you may be feeling, if you remember that you, the Will, the real I AM, is that force which directs the psychic powers to a mental centre in order to cause the brain to become so sensitive that it will respond immediately to your directive. It will respond to such an extent that you can, at will, order it, either to concentrate on this text, or on any other material you may decide to bring before it.

Prayer is one of the finest concentrative exercises, because the brain is directed along a specific predetermined mental channel. We have to concentrate on Prayer in order to be able to say or think it. By concentration in this way, the mind is directed away from the memory of other events, towards the contents of that Prayer. This also causes an explosion of forces not only on the purely mental level but upon the psycho-Spiritual level as well, because directed concentration on the Prayer itself makes a definite demand upon the psychic energy within. This procedure tends to open up some of the psychic centres in the aura a little, so that even a greater energy can be drawn in through these magnetic vortices of Power. We are attracting an extra Power from not only within, but from outside as well, through this applied magnetism. We are then making it into a concentrative force of energy and transmitting it again in a definite way to bring about a result predetermined by the nature of the Prayer. Such a Spiritual practice not only helps the person for whom we pray, but also helps to relieve the psychic frustrations within ourselves. It also tends to sensitize the mind because it tends to cause a balance in the psychic centres so that no specific blockage of psychic energies can later cause psychosomatic troubles.

Prayer is a way to give Spiritual Healing to others. Just as surely, it is a potent way by which each man can give himself a powerful and transmuting balanced form of Healing, because of its direct reaction upon the psychic forces, the psychic centres, the mental forces, as well as a balancing factor on the flow of psychic energies through the subtle and physical nervous systems within the etheric and dense bodies. The frequent use of Prayer can also help man to so control his psychic and mental forces, that he becomes capable of deep sustained concentration (Note 5).

"He can, at this stage, so enhance his concentrative abilities that he is capable of contemplation, with open-minded diligence, which will bring about even greater awareness, a greater understanding and which will begin to open the door of ENLIGHTENMENT."

After some considerable practice in concentration, you then can begin to take the next major step towards Enlightenment which is contemplation. Now, concentration is an active, direct consideration of a particular problem. During concentration, the mind is working continuously towards the solution of that problem. In Prayer, the problem is to send energy from point A—the prayer, to point B—the destination of that Prayer. The mind is active in causing the physical body to reproduce the sound contents of that Prayer while also drawing on the Power within and that outside, so that these energies can be directed in a controlled stream towards the objective. But contemplation, while it begins with concentration, is different in as much as it is not a physically active state, but rather a mental and psychic state. This is the state where the particular problem is actually concentrated upon first and then applied to the mind.

The mind becomes open to receive any particular directive from within, which might have a specific bearing upon the particular problem under consideration. For instance, let us study Prayer again as so little seems to be known about it and yet, there is such a genuine yearning towards its understanding.

Suppose a person discovers that his friend has met with a bad accident. His concentration tells him that, as he is not a medical man, he cannot, by orthodox methods, help his friend. His friend may be in hospital having very fine medical care, but still he desires to help. So he starts to pray in order to direct a stream of Spiritual Power towards the sick friend. This is concentration. In contemplation, he may start praying, but he would also allow the stream of mind substance, which he had attracted towards himself by his specific action, to be translated into, shall we call it, understandable language in his own brain. He would not only send the Power towards his friend, but also receive back from his friend a return flow of energy. The energy he sent to the sick friend may be charged with dynamic good health; the mental energy received back from his hospitalized friend, because of the accident, would be coloured by his sick state and the environment of the hospital. By careful analysis of the stimulus, he would be able to say what was wrong with his friend and what kind of energy was needed to bring about a complete Healing. Here is another illustration. A geologist may look at a piece of rock and say that it is composed of such and such minerals. The geologist would be concentrating upon the rock and would be concluding, by past experience, the composition of the rock. But supposing the geologist was a person capable of contemplation. He would not only concentrate upon the rock, but he would allow his mind to be open, so that he could receive Intuitive information regarding that rock. Then, not only would he know what that rock was composed of, but also where it had come from, and even the character and environment of the person who had picked it up and had given it to him. He would, through his ability to contemplate, be able to give a fairly accurate analysis of the life of the person who had given him the rock, because his mind would be so open, sensitive and aware of the subtler forces of life, that he would be able to "feel" the mental energy pattern of any person who had previously handled the rock. This is contemplation. Some psychics would refer to it as clairvoyance, or psychometry, but both these abilities are really the results of contemplation, for one cannot be a good clairvoyant without being a contemplative; neither can one give a diagnosis of another without taking a contemplation upon that particular person. As well as this, the great psychic forces, which have already been risen by concentration, rise even higher still during contemplation. Even higher psychic centres than those used in concentration are opened during contemplation and through these flow the forces of Intuition (Note 6).

"The next essential step he can then take is the transmutation of mental energies upon the plane of inspiration, called high Intuition. This is brought about by strict control and the manipulation of the individual's Karmic pattern through Service—and so on."

When anyone is able to contemplate correctly, he is then open to receive inspiration. This inspiration is not apparently so much the result of mental deduction, as of psychic awareness which allows the forces of inspiration to become manifest within the contemplative. When this stage is reached, he becomes inspired by the forces of Intuition to such an extent that he becomes knowledgeable. If he strictly controls the Power which is the result of such a condition, he can easily manipulate his own Karmic pattern, because he can give wonderful Service to others. He is capable of the dispensation of a purer form of Love than the person who is only capable of concentration. Such a man then can bring his Karma into a pattern which proves he is then ready to take the next major step towards Enlightenment.

"At this stage he is then capable of Meditation. Through such Meditation the aspirant opens the door even wider, so that the brilliant, everlasting vibration of ENLIGHTENMENT may forever surround him."

Meditation is the next important step of progression. Now, before we can begin to understand Meditation, let us consider, first of all, what this state is not. Meditation is not some vague fluttering flight of concentration, not even a deep psychic state; it is far above all these things. Meditation is only brought about when the all-important Power of Kundalini is risen consciously up the spinal column of the aspirant. It rises from the base Chakra, penetrates the sex centre and moves higher to the solar plexus. As it is moved upwards, it takes all the Power from the sex centre which becomes dormant. It is then moved, consciously, up into the heart centre. As it pierces the heart centre, the solar plexus centre is devoid of its energy and this becomes dormant. At this stage, the Meditator becomes paralyzed, unable to walk. When the Power is taken from the nerve ganglia which act as a Pranic battery in the solar plexus and is risen up to the heart centre, he is no longer able to move his legs and hips. When the Power pierces the heart centre, the Chakra then blossoms forth and the tremendous Power of Love can be, for the first time, understood and radiated to all in need. At this stage, the aspirant is capable of advanced psychic vision. He is able to hear the forces within this vortex of Power. Some of these forces sound to him like a giant bell which is tolling and often he will hear this so loudly, that it will appear to do his ear drums actual physical damage. There is a tremendous strain put upon the centre and, if the heart is weak, it can be damaged by severe palpitation, or, if the student who is raising the Kundalini has not completely controlled the baser aspects of life, he will bring these energies up into the heart centre and cause his heart to be diseased for life. As well as this, if the lower part of his body has some ailment, he will actually transfer the vibrations of this condition to the heart centre and give himself an incurable heart disease. If however, the aspirant has overcome these things and he is then able to raise, consciously, the great Power of Kundalini into the throat centre, the heart centre is, by the magnetic attraction of the Kundalini, devoid of energy and the physical heart nearly stops beating. Now the aspirant is sitting absolutely and completely immobile.

He or she is in a very deep state of trance. The base, sex, solar plexus and heart centres have had all the power taken from them and they are not operating. The aspirant is unable to move physically, because he is completely paralyzed. The blood has almost stopped circulation around the body, because the heart beats have almost ceased, or in some cases, actually physically stopped. The aspirant is, to all intents and purposes, in a state of conscious death. But the Intuition has not stopped. Inner, shining Light and deep vision are being experienced now. Highly elevated mental energies are now being drawn into the throat centre and the Meditator is beginning to understand and appreciate the irrevocable occult Laws for the first time. Inside, there is all vibrant activity. He can hear the tremendous vortex of Power within the Christ Centre above, which physically sounds to him like the rushing waters of a gigantic waterfall. In fact, at first, he cannot hear anything else except this. Then, as he becomes more attuned, he hears the subtle symphony of life. He can hear a tree growing, a man talk to another miles away. He can hear a cloud form 2,000 feet above him if he thinks about it. His hearing becomes so acute that he can hear the subtle sounds of whatever he dwells upon. He can even hear the screeching, high-pitched whine caused by a beam of light as it careers through the envelope of gas molecules which surround the Planet. If he Meditates upon this super-sonic sound, he can become aware of the resonating harmonics, caused as the photons of light are reflected from any object, sounding like a delicately blended symphonic pattern of musical notes which seem, in some strange way, to radiate from all sources at once, yet echo and re-echo as though passing on through some gigantic tunnel.

He can transfer his hearing above the atmospheric belt and hear the strange almost "elongated" sounds of full, vital Space. He becomes a Master of all things audible. He can hear a million notes, most of which he could not name. He could write, if he were consciously able to move that is, great symphonies of Nature's wonderful sounds. He would speak, if he were capable of moving his lips, greater words than Shakespeare—ever wrote.

The aspirant is now an Adept.

If he can now, consciously, raise the Power of Kundalini together with the forces of the throat centre even higher so that the Christ Centre fully opens, he becomes a Master for that time and he is capable of Meditation for 5 minutes, 10 minutes, 50 years, 200 years, it does not matter. His body becomes completely immobile, almost cold. His breathing is barely perceptible. The only heat in the body is a thin band of warmth around the top of the forehead which stops rigor mortis from setting in and this warmth is just enough to keep the blood in a state of semi-suspension.

This is a Metaphysical description of the true Meditative state. This is nothing like the foolish interpretation that ignorant man puts upon it. It is the much sought after state. All states below this are not true Meditative states.

The Adept then becomes one with that upon which he Meditates. When he consciously reverses this flow of Kundalini until it is back down at the base of the spine again, therefore allowing him to use the physical body as he did before, he comes out of this state as a wise and Enlightened person.

"These are the essential steps to ENLIGHTENMENT. There is not an easy path. Some passages are shorter, yet more dangerous, than others. This you know."

There are many eastern Yogic exercises which tend to put tremendous pressures on the nerve centres within the body, thereby enhancing the blood flow around these nerve ganglia so that later, one can bombard the semi-dormant Kundalini with Pranic energies and cause a rise of Kundalini. These passages are shorter, in other words, this is a faster way to gain Enlightenment, which means a rise in Kundalini, but a much more dangerous one. The path outlined in the text, namely that of Service, the dispensation of Love, the conquering of one's lower self, the complete control of mental energies, the control of energies upon the Intuitive level, although not easy, is a longer path than many, but it is the safest one, because it is a carefully balanced one. The Kundalini rises in a more natural, unforced fashion with these particular techniques than with other, more advanced Yogic techniques. Even if the student does decide, against advice, to take the quicker path, he still has to control his lower aspects, strictly control all participation and even thought of sex; he has to make the body fit so that no disease vibrations will be risen upwards, as well as control the mind, the powers of concentration and the psychic forces completely. Even after this, he has to put tremendous pressures upon certain centres in difficult, extremely painful exercises for hours per day in order to cause Kundalini to rise. Even then, there is no guarantee that he will be strong-willed enough to bring Kundalini back to Her base centre again, without mishap.

The shorter paths are indeed the dangerous ones and should NEVER be attempted by laymen without the correct, personal instruction of a Master of Yoga. Total paralysis, madness, incurable diseases can be the result of the faster methods, if taken without the correct, personal supervision of a Master who really understands all the implications of the more difficult exercises. The longer path, through the right Spiritual action, rather than the application of any undue force, is the safest way to cause an activation and eventual rise of Kundalini.

It should always be remembered that, despite all appearances to the contrary, THE COMPLETE CONTROL OF KUNDALINI THROUGH THE SPINAL COLUMN IS MAN'S ONLY REASON FOR BEING ON EARTH, for when this is accomplished, the lessons in this classroom are learned and the mystical examination is passed. This is repeated because of its obvious importance.

"Ignorance is the result of the complication devised by terrestrial man, therefore, ENLIGHTENMENT is simplicity. Use that as the text for your contemplation and eventually, when Meditation is possible, much will be revealed."

This should certainly be used as a focal point for contemplation, for within this text there is great Truth. Try it for yourself—now! (Note 7).

"Note this also: ENLIGHTENMENT cannot dawn while the clouds of indiscrimination cover the skies of your mentality. Discriminate. You have been told how to do this; do it—and go into ENLIGHTENMENT."

The reference here to discrimination is extremely important. If you travel along one of the many false paths, which will only lead you into a cul-de-sac, then you will have to come back from where you left the main path of Truth and start all over again. There are many false teachers and false prophets in these days (Note 8).

Discrimination is brought about by applied logic. You may ask why is this so important as, according to the ancient Bible called the *Bhagavad Gita*, it is better to follow a "false god" than it is to follow no God at all. This is true, but why waste valuable time studying a false teaching when there are enlightening teachings virtually cast at your feet?

As this is a Metaphysical textbook some definite pointers which will guide your discriminations will not be amiss at this stage. Let us, for example, take what is undoubtedly the foremost source of true Metaphysical teachings in these days and indeed has been throughout history, namely those teachings which are delivered by Higher

Intelligences from other Planets.

There are very few people living upon this Earth who have regular contacts with Cosmic Intelligences! There are some people who have been contacted at one time or another, but note, there are very few REGULAR contacts between Cosmic Masters and this Earth. You should always inquire of someone claiming regular contact with Cosmic sources, as to the period of training he underwent beforehand. If the claimant had no training at all in this life, then you would be safe in keeping away from him or her entirely in case you are following a false contact or one being deluded by astral entities, using an Earth channel who, because of his ignorance of the difficult process of communication and obvious lack of experience, is unable to raise his consciousness to such a high level that only the real Cosmic Masters and not those impersonating them, could speak. There is not one genuine, regular mental channel on this Earth, known to the writer who has not had to undergo years of difficult, intensive Yogic training under the strictest self discipline in this life, before he or she could be used as the medium through which Cosmic Truths are conveyed to mankind. Never forget, that even great Masters like Jesus and Buddha had, in their historical lives upon Earth, to take special intensive training. Buddha for at least 10 years and Jesus for even longer—practised Yoga, mainly in Northern India and Thibet, before They gave Their Teachings to Earth. Even though the author considers himself as naught in comparison with truly Enlightened Beings like these, nevertheless They set a pattern for him to follow and a pattern also to help you to discriminate between the genuine and the deluded. Think about that. Talk to everyone claiming to be the mouthpiece of any Master, whether terrestrial or Interplanetary. If he is an ignorant man, then leave him at once. Every true contact must, of necessity, have to be well versed in applied Metaphysics and practical occultism before he can be chosen as a regular contact. If any "contactee" claims to be given information in a trance condition, ASK HIM TO DESCRIBE THIS CONDITION IN PURE METAPHYSICAL LANGUAGE. If he cannot do this, or says something vague like: "Oh, I just go into a trance," be careful because he is probably the victim of delusion. Read very carefully every alleged Space Message which comes through each individual. If these teachings are based upon the deeper aspects of the Ancient occult Truths, then heed them. If they are not, then leave them alone. If a so-called "space master" speaks only from a purely orthodox Christian point of view, then he is less knowledgeable than an advanced Earth occultist, never mind one from the Higher Spheres.

A real Space Messenger would speak in such a way that it proved He understood the philosophies propounded by Avatars, Who started all major Religions. He would certainly praise true Christianity, but also Buddhism as well. Such an Intelligence would remind you that Shri-Krishna was a more advanced Master than even Buddha or Jesus.

No legitimate Space Contact has ever yet said that, "Jesus is in control of a huge fleet of Space Vessels, which would come to the assistance of the West in a war with the communists." If you hear such a thing, leave that "channel" severely alone. Note this, Intelligences from other Planets do not agree with war, nor the present political system adopted by any country in the world today. They do not agree with the present economic system. They certainly disagree, and have bluntly stated so in many instances, with the use of atomic energy as a murder weapon (Note 9).

If any alleged "message" purporting to come from an Interplanetary Intelligence is entirely materialistic and tells you to leave the Spiritual and Metaphysical approach to Truth entirely alone—drop it, for it is an evil fake. If you read or hear of an Interplanetary contact, whether mental or supposedly physical, which states: "Jesus was not an advanced Avatar, because He could not save Himself from the cross," this will be the classic example of, not only a fake, but a force evil enough to try to belittle One of the most wonderful Masters ever to walk the Earth. If any so-called terrestrial "contactee" states that he has spent some days on another Planet in a physical body attending a "supreme council meeting," disregard him, for no Earth man has yet done such a thing. The present text will teach you why such a statement would be absolutely ridiculous and untrue. If any claims are made of a contact, either mental or physical, with the Logos of Earth, the Sun Lords or the Lord of any Planet, Star or Galaxy, you should totally disregard such claims because no Being of this calibre would ever need to contact a terrestrial. If any Metaphysical teacher falls short of any of the pointers given herein, then to be absolutely safe, you should leave him and his alleged "message" severely alone.

You might save yourself the pain of retracing your steps from the cul-de-sac where you are being wrongly led, because the retracing of these steps may take you a long time.

These are the ways in which you should discriminate if you are ever to enjoy Enlightenment. Some may ask:"If one man says this and the other says that, how do I know which is right?" Follow both of them in the beginning and study carefully what both have to say. The wrong one will prove that he is wrong and the right one will, if you are open-minded enough, prove to you that he is right.

Truth will live—lies will fall sooner or later. If you apply the advice given herein, if you diligently study the author's recommendations and make these true Teachings your pattern, you will be able to differentiate between the genuine and the fake. Look at The Nine Freedoms, look how profound, how all-embracing these great Truths are. There is nothing petty in them, is there? These genuine teachings tell the whole world how to live, how to gain Enlightenment, the essential steps in Evolutionary progression. This is another measure of Truth which is impersonal and is always given to the whole world instead of only to a small group of individuals.

Use these pointers as your yardstick, apply this knowledge to the majority of so-called "messages" allegedly coming from the Masters and you will see that, only a small minority are then left when you have completed the sorting out process. The reason for this advice on discrimination is not to condemn others, even if they are known to be false, but to help you—the genuine searcher, so that you can save yourself the pain of bitter disappointment brought on by being led astray by falsehood and basic psychic delusion.

"While you slip like one of your animals, from place to place, chewing here and there, you will not gain ENLIGHTENMENT."
This is very true. When once you have found the right track, you must stick to it, no matter how difficult it appears to be. Remember, you cannot gain full Enlightenment quickly or easily.

"I have instructed you before to choose well, then stand fast in order to know God. This you must be prepared to do."
When you have applied the yardstick of logical discrimination and chosen your teacher you must be prepared to stand fast. You must remain unflinchingly loyal, treating your lessons as priceless gems of Sacred Wisdom and not allow yourself to be swayed by petty dislikes which all too often hold up your progress. If your choice has been a good one, your teacher will show you the path of Service. Follow this and in time you will begin to realize the tremendous potential with-

in you. Then you will begin to go surely towards Enlightenment and a deep realization of the God Powers within.

"Note this, I speak of Freedom—not petty freewill. There is a God of difference."

It is the petty freewill, the foolish likes and dislikes of mankind which have imprisoned him. While he is ruled by these, he cannot know Freedom. He must be prepared to give up his petty freewill in order to know Freedom. Go back to the paragraph on concentration and you will see that you can never concentrate unless you make up your mind to control the vague wanderings of your thoughts. You can never contemplate unless you have mastered the art of concentration. You will never, not in this or any future life, be able to Meditate, until you have completely mastered your powers of concentration and contemplation to such an extent that you consciously impose tremendous physical and mental limitations upon yourself, in order to gain Freedom, for that is the difference between petty freewill and Freedom. The text states quite definitely: *"There is a God of difference."*

True realization will eventually teach you the vast difference between these two states.

"Serve, manipulate your Karmic pattern, then you will be allowed to walk through the dawn of ENLIGHTENMENT."

If you serve in all the ways which are mentioned herein, you will manipulate your Karmic pattern to such an extent that, by Law, you will have proved yourself ready to advance to those elevated states of consciousness which bring, as their lasting reward, the much sought after prize called—Enlightenment.

AUTHOR'S RECOMMENDATIONS

NOTE 1. Study and practice of the correctly balanced, mystic breathing methods given in, *Your Higher Self Through Yoga*, will help in the control of Universal Life Forces.

NOTE 2. Read the Metaphysical lessons, *Man's Mind,* and *Imagination— Your Only Creative Faculty,* and also *The Pendulum—How Does It Work?* for a deeper understanding of the Power and function of the human mind.

NOTE 3. All students are strongly recommended to carefully study the Metaphysical lessons, *Control Of The Vital Life Fluid,* and *Secret Of*

Dynamic Absent Healing. These form a basis for all Metaphysical studies.

NOTE 4. Study *Concentration—Contemplation—Meditation*, for the Metaphysical outline of these essential steps towards Enlightenment.

NOTE 5. A close study and practice of the Metaphysical lessons, *Dynamic Prayer Brings Results*, and *The Secret Of Dynamic Absent Healing*, together with other literature recommended elsewhere in *The Nine Freedoms*, will teach the serious student a great deal about the theory and practice of Divine or Prayer Healing.

NOTE 6. A study of, *How To Develop Your Clairvoyant Powers*, will be of great help to all students.

NOTE 7. Read "Cosmic Logic," in *You Are Responsible!* (pages 110-116) for a brilliant reference to simplicity as given by a Cosmic Master.

NOTE 8. Discrimination is of the utmost importance to the Metaphysical student. The following reading matter is deemed an essential minimum: *Cosmic Voice* Issue No. 23 (pages 1-3), *You Are Responsible!* (pages 145-159). *Discrimination*, a Metaphysical lesson devoted entirely to this important subject. *Trance—Its Various Types*, is another specially prepared lesson highly recommended as an aid to all important discrimination.

NOTE 9. The following carefully selected reading matter will give the serious humanitarian student a better working knowledge of the opinions expressed by Higher Authority on the dangers of atomic experimentation. "The Challenge Of The H-Bomb," in *Cosmic Voice Volume No. 1* (pages 80-83) and *Cosmic Voice Volume No. 2* (pages 103-104). "Co-Existence," in *Cosmic Voice Volume No. 2* (pages 91-92), "Greatest Happenings Of Modern Times," in *Cosmic Voice Volume No. 2* (pages 32-34). "Be Sane Ye Men," in *Cosmic Voice Issue No. 25* (pages 10-12). "Power From Jupiter Saves Earth," in *Cosmic Voice Issue No. 25* (pages 29-33). "You Are Responsible," in *Wisdom Of The Planets*. "The Dangers Of the H-Bomb," in *You Are Responsible!* (pages 86-103).

All the above recommended books and lessons are obtainable from the publishers of *The Nine Freedoms*.

As a supplementary study the advanced student should read, *Natures Finer Forces* (pages 32-95) and *The Science Of Breath* (pages 201-253). This book is written by Rama Prasad and published by the Theosophical Publishing House, Adyar, Madras, India (1933). Possibly obtainable from any branch of the Theosophical Society.

THE THIRD SATELLITE

The Third Satellite is a colossal Spacecraft controlled by the Martian Adept—Mars Sector 6. This comes into an orbit of Earth for several periods each year, the dates of which are always given beforehand and published in Aetherius Society material. The periods of these orbits are called, "Magnetization Periods." During a "Magnetization Period," all truly selfless Spiritual activities performed on behalf of mankind are potentized exactly 3,000 times because of the highly concentrated and carefully balanced energy waves radiated from Satellite No. 3. So finely are these energies combined and manipulated by the expert Astro-Metaphysicians on the Spacecraft, that never can they be used wrongly or for selfish purposes.

The Satellite is totally invisible to physical human eyes and it cannot be detected by radar.

Invisibility of the Satellite is brought about by revolving the photons, which would normally be emanated by light reflection from the hull of the craft, in a 360 degree arc within the magnetic force screen around the vessel.

The Satellite cannot be detected by terrestrial radar because the particle emission radiated through the radar antenna is not allowed to be reflected after collision with the mass of the vessel. These energies are absorbed into a special screen around the Spacecraft thereby making radar detection impossible.

There are good reasons for the Space Intelligences adopting both of these precautions. It should be pointed out that when any energy is reflected by an object, the energy particles are, to some degree, conditioned by that mass through collision. So minutely exact are the energy radiations from Satellite No. 3 that their delicate balance and predetermined results would be upset by normal light reflection and certainly by radar pulse reflection.

It is difficult for ordinary Earth brains to fully appreciate a science as exact as that practised on Satellite No. 3, but careful study and applied common sense will soon tell you that in order to be able to clearly predetermine a psycho-Spiritual result, all interfering factors must be eliminated from the chain of progress which eventually leads up to that result.

All the following drawings of Satellite No. 3 were done under the supervision of the author who visited this Spacecraft, for the first time, on March 23rd, 1956 (See Chapter 6).

PLATE 3. This shows the egg shaped Spacecraft as it would look if it were visible from just above the surface of Earth.

The Sun's rays, or Pranas, enter through the large crystalline window in the top of the craft. As well as being a collector of Solar energies, this dome also acts as a filter so that any aspect of energy which is needed can be isolated and controlled by the operators of the vessel. The energies are then radiated through the precisely made matrix at the bottom of the vehicle.

PLATE 4. Shows the orbit of the Satellite 1,550 miles above the Earth.

PLATE 5. The Universal Life Forces emitted from the Sun enter through the large crystalline filter in the top of the giant instrument and are isolated by the three prisms. Each of these prisms is over 7 feet tall. They are specially cultivated as individual crystals.

The isolated energies are then further conditioned by absorption into and radiation through the huge ovoid transmitting crystal. Despite the fact that this ovoid is about 30 feet high, it is not suspended from the domed roof of the craft. Neither is it supported from the floor, but it "floats" immobile in the Operations Room apparently defying the known laws of gravity.

PLATE 6. This graph illustrates the average units of energy used by all Spiritual workers throughout the world during each "Magnetization Period." This information is always given by Mars Sector 6 during the last hour of every "Magnetization Period" just prior to the vacation of terrestrial orbit by the Satellite.

It can be seen that the two highest peaks on the graph were attained during the delivery of "The Twelve Blessings" by the Master Jesus and The Nine Freedoms, by Mars Sector 6, Himself. In comparing these two readings it should be noted that Satellite No. 3 was in orbit almost throughout the delivery of "The Twelve Blessings," whereas it did not come into orbit until just prior to the beginning of The Fourth Freedom. All the energy radiated while the first three Freedoms were being delivered was not taken into account in the computation of the nine units of absorption shown on the graph. It should also be noted that all figures given are computed by Interplanetary Intelligences as a world average. During every

"Magnetization Period" Mars Sector 6 arranges "Special Power Transmissions" during which time as much as 1,000 units of Power are put through individuals who cooperate throughout the world. In addition to this, millions of units are channelled through three specially trained Interplanetary Adepts now on Earth. Even after such fantastic Power is channelled to Earth, the average absorption or use, may be as low as 5 or 6 units. Why? Because most of the energy has been reflected rather than absorbed and used by most of the inhabitants on Earth. If, for example, the average Spiritual calibre of every one in the world was equal to that of most of the men and women who form the groups of The Aetherius Society cooperators during a "Special Power Transmission," then, of course, the average energy absorption factor would easily be up in the hundreds. Such figures would mean that mankind, on the whole, would prove himself to be scores of times more advanced than he is at the present time.

There is much to be learned by a close study of this graph. The ebb and flow of world conditions, caused by the greed of some and permitted by the laziness and complacency of others, has its reflection in the peaks and valleys caused by the unstable Power absorption factors shown clearly in the graph. Hence the vital importance of Spiritual Service to others, a rare calling, yet one emphasized by all true Avatars, as being the ONLY SURE PATH TO TERRESTRIAL SALVATION as well as personal Evolution.

These explanations and drawings should give students some idea of the immeasurable importance of the wholly unselfish task continually being performed by the truly exalted Being—Mars Sector 6 and His team of Interplanetary experts on Satellite No. 3.

Remember—every true act of service to another, every unselfish Prayer uttered for the benefit of a stranger or mankind as a whole, is potentized 3,000 times during the time that Satellite No. 3 is in orbit of Earth! Such is the quality and importance of the work done by those on this Spacecraft.

During the time Satellite No. 3 circles around Earth, every minute of your life presents another chance to cooperate with a Master Plan designed to bring lasting world peace and glorious Enlightenment to all.

No one whose thoughts are motivated by common humanitarian decency, never mind lofty Spiritual ambition, will want to waste one fleeting precious second of this, their Divine opportunity to assist the

Great Ones to bring into living, vital manifestation, God's omnipotent Plan for the Cosmic progress of all men.

AUTHOR'S RECOMMENDATIONS

Further information about the activities and work of The Third Satellite may be had by reading the following:

"Importance Of Power Absorption," in *Cosmic Voice* Issue No. 21 (pages 13-14).

"First Transmission In U.S.A.," in *Cosmic Voice* Issue No. 21 (pages 17-19).

"Use This Vital Power," in *Cosmic Voice* Issue No. 22 (pages 24-25).

"Action Is Essential," in *Cosmic Voice* Issue No. 25 (pages 3-8).

"From Freewill To Freedom," in *Cosmic Voice* Issue No. 25 (pages 25-26).

"Emergency Operations," in *Cosmic Voice* Issue No. 25 (inside back cover).

"Power From Jupiter Saves Earth," in *Cosmic Voice* Issue No. 26 (pages 29-33).

All obtainable from the publishers of *The Nine Freedoms*.

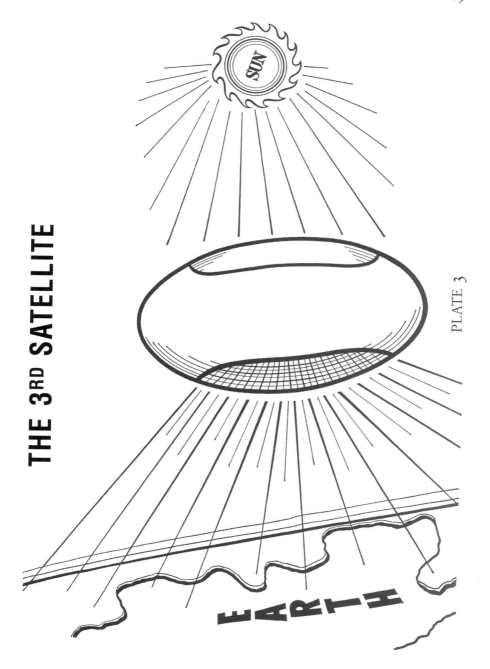

THE 3RD SATELLITE

PLATE 3

THE ORBIT OF THE
3RD SATELLITE

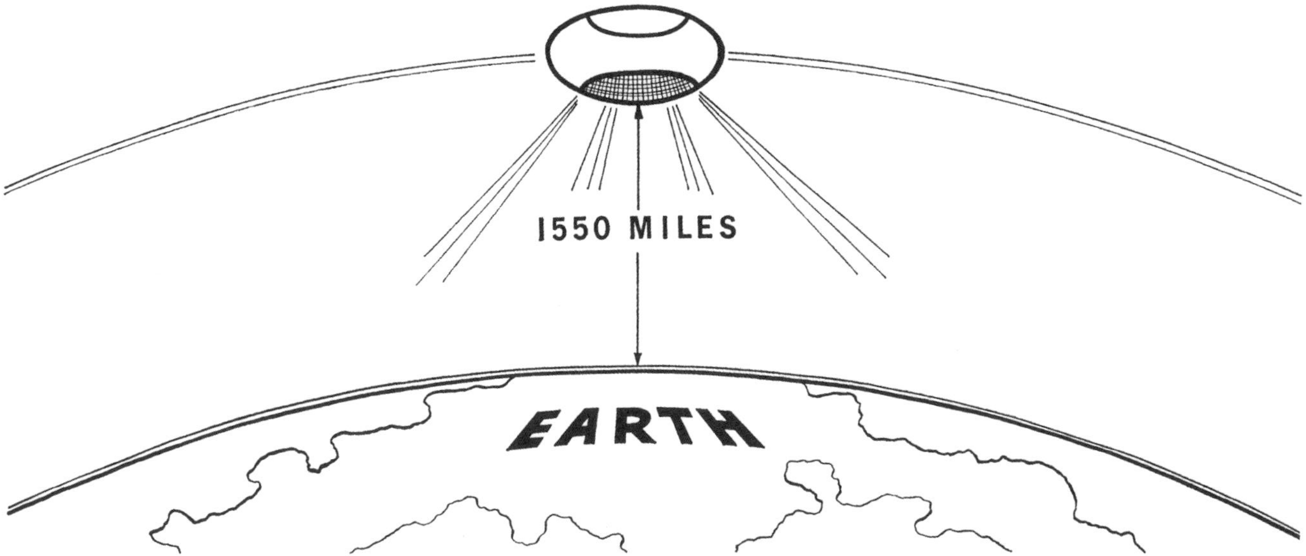

EARTH

1550 MILES

PLATE 4

INSIDE THE 3RD SATELLITE

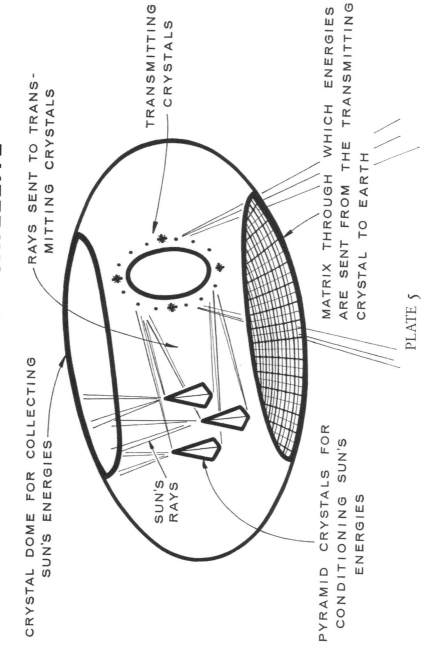

TRANSMITTING CRYSTALS

RAYS SENT TO TRANS- MITTING CRYSTALS

MATRIX THROUGH WHICH ENERGIES ARE SENT FROM THE TRANSMITTING CRYSTAL TO EARTH

CRYSTAL DOME FOR COLLECTING SUN'S ENERGIES

SUN'S RAYS

PYRAMID CRYSTALS FOR CONDITIONING SUN'S ENERGIES

PLATE 5

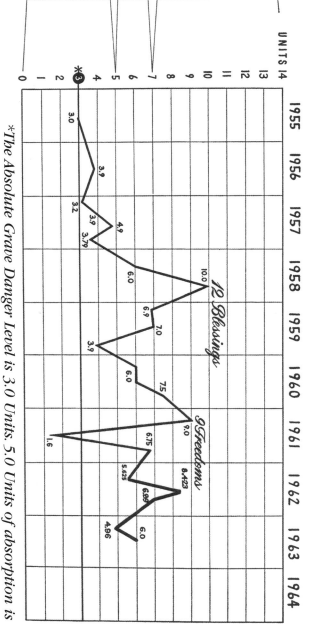

POWER ABSORBED BY SPIRITUAL WORKERS DURING MAGNETIZATION PERIODS

*The Absolute Grave Danger Level is 3.0 Units. 5.0 Units of absorption is still only on the fringe of the Danger Level.

PLATE 6

CHAPTER 5

THE FIFTH FREEDOM WILL BE COSMIC CONSCIOUSNESS

SAINT GOO-LING

"By Power vested in Me, I Bless this Prasad in sacrifice to Brahma. I Bless whole in sacrifice to Brahma.

"Afterwards dispense Prasad to all and eat as sacrifice to everlasting Brahma.

"Now, again, same Intelligence will give another Freedom, during this time you will be used as channels for Power radiation which will be of great benefit to your country for reasons I have already stated.

"Relax and let Power flow through you. Do not let your curiosity hold up this Power.

"I go."

MARS SECTOR 6

"This is Mars Sector 6 reporting from Satellite No. 3, now in Magnetization Orbit—Terra, during Magnetization Period No. 1, present phase.

"The Fifth Freedom will be—COSMIC CONSCIOUSNESS.

"Freedom from limitations is only brought about by sincere and diligent, directed effort through countless incarnations upon Terra. It is not some vague thing which just happens, it is made to happen.

"Terra is a great classroom to which pupils have come to learn many lessons.

"They pass from grade to grade, through countless Initiations, through countless apparent deaths, when they cast off gross physical limitation for a time and travel to another more subtle plane to learn. Then to return again to benefit from their previous experiences.

93

"There comes a stage when the desire to break forever the bars of selfishness dawns—Service is performed.

"There comes a following stage when Enlightenment, like a Sun, doth flood the server with its golden light—Wisdom dawns.

"There comes a stage when, at once, the consciousness of the individual soars to mighty heights, unlimited, unbounded by mind. High into the realms of Intuition, of Divine Inspiration it goeth. Through Space, where time stands quite still, non-existent, immobile.

"COSMIC CONSCIOUSNESS, like the flower of God, breaks from a bud into full, lasting bloom. No longer does such a one regard itself as this sex or the other, for it is above such limitation. No longer does such a one take foolish pride in being born this race or the other, for it knoweth that it is a part of all the races.

"From the very depths it came unto this stage and now, it begins a great and mighty journey through Cosmic Truth.

"This is the real beginning of Freedom, for freewill is recognized for what it is, binding, breaking, individual. It is transmuted into That—which is collective, all embracing, knowing, changing, but this change above time. This change into—Cosmic Wisdom.

"Indeed is this the step to lasting Freedom. And at its zenith—what—continuance? Nay, this the great test. At its zenith—detachment through every stage back to limitation.

"This is the essence of Adeptship, not acceptance as much as detachment. So the Adept detaches, taking from his glorious, violet head, the golden crown of COSMIC CONSCIOUSNESS, to leave it in the Supra mind belt.

"Again through Service doth he go. Again to taste the ecstatic glory of expansion. Expansion which knoweth no human limitation. Expansion through a body and all bodies. Through a World and all Worlds. Through a plane and all planes. All existent. Within the lasting timelessness of—Now.

"Like a voice of a great God—soundless—yet all sound—is this Freedom.

"Terrestrial man is continually limiting these latent abilities within his real self. He is continually imposing limitation after limitation upon these glorious aspects of True Creation. What is the result?

Racial prejudice, adherence and vain worship of some piece of multi-coloured cloth, possession and family tie. He does not realize and cannot fully realize, until after lives of Service, that no one is a nearer relative to him than his enemy. He does not realize that he is a cell in the body of the Cosmic Whole until he has gained the Four Freedoms.

"Take these steps, oh brothers of Earth.

"Break from materialistic bondage and limitation and go ye into the dawn of COSMIC CONSCIOUSNESS—for, by this move, you prove your readiness for even a greater step.

"Know that within you burns a Flame, an all-knowing Flame, an all-existent Flame, a Flame which is neither here nor there, a Flame which is neither hot nor cold, a Flame which is neither light nor darkness and yet all of these. A Flame which is not mind—and yet is all-knowing. A Flame which knoweth no limitation—and yet, vaguely, recognizes individuality.

"The Spark of God resides in man, untouched, until man takes this Cosmic step. Even then, he toucheth not this Flame, but liveth, with all feeling, through its brilliant radiations—light—which passeth mere foolish, verbose description and yet, is passive.

"Know this: when the two flowers of the heart are fed and sleep; when the three flowers of the head are fed and go inwards; and the middle sentinel remains silent; then doth the dawn of the consciousness, which is Cosmic, break and you become at one with—That which Is.

"You are then ready to go to—Freedom.

"Transmute limitation in the four fires and enjoy the light of the Fifth.

"All Transmissions are now discontinued."

Delivered on Wednesday, March 1st, 1961.

COSMIC CONSCIOUSNESS

"During this time, you will be used as channels for Power radiation which will be of great benefit to your country for reasons I have already stated."

Again Saint Goo-Ling reminded the invited audience who attended The Nine Freedoms, that they were being used as channels for a very definite type of energy which was manipulated by The Cosmic Powers at the same time that profound Wisdom was given to Earth. The nature of this energy is explained in the previous chapter.

"Relax and let Power flow through you. Do not let your curiosity hold up this Power."

This advice by Saint Goo-Ling has a deep occult significance. It is a certain fact that Spiritual Power cannot flow easily along the sheaths of the human nervous system while there is tension in the nerves and the muscular systems through which those nerves travel. The only way to have an unimpeded flow of Spiritual Power through you is to physically relax so that it may be allowed to flow.

The reference made to curiosity holding up the flow of this energy was obvious advice to the audience to take no notice of what was actually happening before them, namely the deep Yogic Samadhic condition attained by the author during this time, but to try to heighten their consciousness to such a level that they appreciated the higher procedures while not taking any notice of the physical happenings which were taking place. This type of detachment can be learned. There are some people who, when they attend a profound lecture, close their eyes so that they may give the words of the speaker their full concentration. This procedure is a good one as it helps to give undivided attention to what is being said. While the eyes are open and perceiving different happenings, the mind tends to dart from the perception of the eyes back to what is being heard and back again to where the eyes are focused so that you cannot give your undivided, concentrated attention to what is being said.

The main reason for inviting the audience to hear The Nine Freedoms being initially given was so that each of them could be used as a channel for the energy which was manipulated, rather than hear what was being said at that time. Saint Goo-Ling reminded them all in a very gentle but nevertheless definite manner, of their responsibilities.

"The Fifth Freedom will be—COSMIC CONSCIOUSNESS."

"Freedom from limitation is only brought about by sincere and diligent directed effort through countless incarnations upon Terra. It is not some vague thing which just happens, it is made to happen."

There is no doubt that mankind has put numerous limitations upon himself. There is also no doubt that he is present, in the classroom called Earth, to learn to take off these limitations. The Soul of man is as a bright light which has been covered by numerous different coloured materials. The light which now shines from the Soul, through the thought and action of man, is a different colour from the pure radiance which is the source. As he strips limitations from himself, or layers of material from this light, so it changes colour with each one taken off and it gradually becomes brighter and purer, until there will come a time when it will shine with its original, unadulterated, white radiance through all his thoughts and actions. At this time, man will be much nearer to God than he is at present.

The limitations imposed by man upon himself have certain, very direct results, which manifest in his every thought and action. Definite steps must be taken in order to balance these thoughts and actions and overcome the self-imposed limitations, so that man can rise into his full dominion. The statement: "It is made to happen" means that limitation can only be transmuted in the fires of right thought and action through sustained effort. No other forces in this Universe can accomplish for any of you as much as you can for yourself. All that the Masters can do is to advise you of the path to be taken and then it is up to you to take this path, providing you are ready to strip from your limited self the imposed limitations. If you are not ready to make this effort, then you will stay just where you are—behind the bars of the prison of your own making. This choice, purely an individual one, must be taken sooner or later by all men. If it is taken at this time, much pain can be avoided. If it is left to a later date, then the experiences which are necessary in order to strip from the light of the Soul the discolouration which you have put there may be very painful ones.

"COSMIC CONSCIOUSNESS, like the flower of God, breaks from a bud into full, lasting bloom. No longer does such a one regard itself as this sex or the other, for it is above such limitation."

When the complete control has been brought about over the great primeval Fires of Kundalini, when "She" has been moved through the spinal column many times, when you, through single-minded, undeviating effort, have attained the deep state of Meditation and can indeed attain this state at will, you so prepare the lower and higher consciousness for even a deeper state of awareness—that of Cosmic Consciousness. This elevated condition is one of the ultimate results of Meditation and indeed is the goal which can only be attained in the very deepest of these states. Very little has ever been written about Cosmic Consciousness for it is the truth that only those who have experienced it can have any conception of what it is really like, and even then a full description defies any words.

COSMIC CONSCIOUSNESS AS RELATED FROM AN ACTUAL EXPERIENCE.

Deep breath. The tides of Universal Life Force were drawn in, to be directed along the singing nerve sheaths by concentrated mind and thrown down hard to the base of the spine, there to be risen by mind, which knew only one objective—that of complete Mastery over the latent Powers within. Powers, which just awaited the key, the chord, to bring them into active, vibrant movement. Tremendous effort— and then "She," this great mysterious Goddess—Kundalini, which all men strive to raise, did move. This time though, apparently easier and even more surely than "She" had before. It was as though "She," in Her grace, had decided that this was some Divine and auspicious occasion.

Gently at first, creeping almost like a snake, "She" came upwards and ever upwards. The burning sensation in the base of the spine, which had been felt many times before, was experienced this time, but as if the Gods Themselves were standing guard over the Adept, his detachment from the excruciating pain was even more complete than ever it had been before. "She" moved gently upwards and when "She" pierced the solar plexus centre, even though his eyes were closed to the world, he could see more surely than ever he had when those eyes were physically opened.

He struggled on and gradually moved Her through the solar plexus—climbing, creeping slowly, gently, yet as sure as the Light of the Sun, did he bring Her upwards. Great rivers of perspiration streamed down his face and neck even though he was so cold he could have wept. Though he could not move one leg, he shook as though afflicted with ague when his spine vibrated in sympathy with the tremendously powerful rising forces. When, after what seemed an age of shaking mental agony, in all Her grace "She" dwelt within the heart centre, his vision was extended. No longer was the world built of gross physical matter, but had a strangely subtle pattern which normal man could not appreciate. No longer did a colour stand alone, but was surrounded by musical tones which went resonating into the distance. Yet, those ears could hear them even to the farthest ends of this distance.

His vision was extended through the place he was in and beyond. It was as though he had all-seeing vision. Mysteries which had remained, to this day, like ancient charts lost beneath the ocean of forgetfulness came before his eyes and he saw, read and understood them.

Then, steadfast, not content with even this, he fervently fought for Her added grace to climb even further upwards.

And "She" came.

When "She" entered the throat centre, he sat immobile as one in physical death, yet pulsating with greater life than he had ever experienced before. As "She" entered and dwelt within the throat centre, "She" lent to this Her grace and Power and his world became one of sound as well as vision. A million sounds were appreciated. Those nerves within his body which were still alive, thrilled to the exotic, symphonic harmony of Nature—Itself. He felt, at that time, he was one with Nature; but was soon to find that this was just a small beginning.

The great Power rose upwards. As though by the grace of some invisible, but merciful God, "She" rose, slowly, surely, creeping ever upwards, taking him into even higher realms than this. Then—all of a sudden—"She" emerged from the top of the spine and in a glorious flash, the Christ Centre was open. He began to know who he was and why he came. At this time, immobile, cold as if dead, he experienced even a greater life than most men have ever dreamed of and yet, in some strange way, was detached from it all. It was as though, he, a Light, was alone in the Universe. It was as though he, at this moment, was being probed by a radiant beam of exploring intelligence, so intense, so ancient, so wise, that It knew his every movement from his initial birth a million, million years ago until this day, aye, and even beyond that to some dim part of the future, so distant as to be beyond even his enhanced comprehension. The great Light shone apparently through him to almost, what was to the Adept, infinity and seemed, in some strange way, to return to him with the Wisdom of the Ages collected by its immense journey.

As the great Goddess of Power dwelt within this Chakra the Adept, in true deep Meditation, became a knower. He felt that this state, despite his complete aloneness—was the ultimate. He knew later that this feeling was but an expression of his ignorance, for suddenly, even as a great shock to him, this great Power reached to the upper most branch of the tree and then, gradually at first, but surely, the highest centre opened.

It was as though in a moment, he wore above his head a crown of indescribable magnificence!

A glorious brilliant flash of illumination came to him.

The Powers before were nothing in comparison with this. Oh God, he was going even further upwards.

His loneliness subsided, as a calm will stop the turbulence of the waves at sea and peace began—but not static peace, for in this was all movement. He began to stretch outwards as though he had immense arms which were embracing all things. His consciousness reached outwards—holding and gradually came the realization of oneness. No longer was he a Light in the wilderness as he had been before, but now he was an essential part, an intimate part, an inter-related part of all things. His consciousness soared above the environment, above the city in which his cold body sat immobile, around the city, around all things and all people and all environments. Soaring upwards and outwards, he was now in the full and complete realization that he was Life, which was manifesting in countless different ways in order to gain the experience necessary, the control demanded over matter itself. Here, in such an elevated state as this, came a deeper realization than ever before, of the interrelationship of all things, of the Life of all things. When he dwelt, for a moment, upon a rock, it sprang into vibrant life before his "Eye." It breathed, it had feeling, it had disappointment. The rock, in some vague way, experienced passion, it had a Soul, a veritable Spiritual essence which linked it with him, with all. As the state became even more advanced, he felt as though he was above the world embracing it all, a part of it. Living with it in complete intimacy, knowing it, appreciating it, loving it as he had never felt Love before. He became one with that upon which his Super-Consciousness dwelt. He became detached from this one-ness when he felt he should, in order to learn from the experience of detachment and attached when he wanted to in order to learn from the experience of attachment.

He became existent in timelessness.

He became vitally aware of the dimensions in which he existed and knew them—aye, all seven of them. He became as tiny as a mol-ecule when he wanted to and yet bigger than a world when he wished. He looked down from his lofty position high above the Earth, appreciating Its great glory, Its Power, Its supreme Light; perceiving the limitations It had put upon Itself in order to allow lifestreams, like him, to gain the very experience which he was now living through in almost Godlike ecstasy. It was then, when this realization dawned, that he stopped short.

Here was the very Power which he had sought. Power beyond the wildest dreams, beyond the most imaginative conception of mere man; Power to know what secrets he wished; Power greater than that needed to move any mountain, anywhere, at any time. But yet, he stopped short as though strangely disappointed with himself. Beneath him, beneath the crust of Earth, within the Ancient Globe dwelt a greater Being than he or all men. A Being which had imposed upon Itself, crushing limitations, so that the mass of men could crawl through existence upon Its back in order to gain experience, knowl-edge and eventually—even Wisdom.

It was as though he had learned the great lesson brought about by striving for this, what was to him then, an ultimate state of being. The lesson of detachment from even the greatest states he learned and gradually he came back, becoming smaller and smaller with every true Spiritual desire. Gradually he crept away from his all powerful state—slowly diminishing, until again he became the lonely Light shining through Space. He dimmed this as he brought the Power of Kundalini downwards. As he descended the ladder from the lofty heights of Cosmic Consciousness, when Kundalini passed through the throat centre, he became aware again of the world of sonic vibra-tions. He was tempted to linger here, but the haunting vision of that wonderful Being, which was the Earth, suffering gross limitation to be the world, to be a sure home for crawling ignorant man who would be lost in Space without Her, caused him to leave the ecstasy of this sound plane and downwards came the Kundalini until he became aware again of his coarse physical structure and of his gross limitations, of his cold shivering body and stiff aching limbs (Note 1).

Indeed is the text right when it states: *"No longer does such a one regard itself as this sex or the other, for it is above such limitation."*

In true Cosmic Consciousness, sex is regarded as a necessary polarity which must be experienced by male and female alike so that each lifestream may gain essential knowledge from both sets of experiences.

"No longer does such a one take foolish pride in being born this race or the other, for it knoweth that it is a part of all the races."

Those few people who have ever experienced true Cosmic Consciousness know, beyond all doubt, that they are inter-related one with another. They are fully aware that they are but an expression of the One Life which is manifesting Itself through the different sexes, colours and races in order to gain the all essential experience as it gradually makes its way back to its Divine Source. Such a one as this no longer takes pride in being born in this country or that, but rather says with a strong inner conviction: "I belong to the one race of Life!"

"From the very depths it came unto this stage and now, it begins a great and mighty journey through Cosmic Truth."

In the beginning, the One Divine Creative Source or, The Absolute, saw fit to involve Itself in Its own created materialism. It saw fit to individualize Itself. It saw fit to send forth a million, million parts of Itself and involve these in gross matter, so that each part would make its way back to the Pure State which existed before manifestation. This is the deepest philosophy, the greatest Truth, the only answer possible to man for the very existence of Evolution. There never has been a Truth advanced, which is more logical than this, neither can any philosophy dispute these facts, even though neither man nor Master can say why this is so—only that it must be.

"Indeed is this the step to lasting Freedom. And at its zenith— what—continuance? Nay, this the great test. At its zenith—detachment through every stage back to limitation."

This, as Mars Sector 6 wisely states, is the essence of true Adeptship. To strive hard for a highly elevated state, learn what that state can teach and then learn detachment from that state back to limitation, so that the fruits of Cosmic Consciousness can be given to others who are searching for the food of Truth in the garden of Wisdom. Only the greatest have ever realized this aspect of Truth. The Master has, many times in The Nine Freedoms, stressed this procedure and in so doing, He has put the indelible stamp of greatness upon Himself, for this Truth is the subtlety of lasting Wisdom. Even as the author learned, beyond any doubt, during his actual experience of Cosmic Consciousness, narrated earlier in this chapter, that the Goddess, which is this Earth, was bearing limitation so that man could profit through it, so also, in a smaller way, did he have to impose limitations upon himself, so that you could profit, through a study of the report of his actual experiences. Had he not chosen to impose the limitation of detachment from the elevated state of Cosmic Consciousness, then the world, as such, could not have profited through his experience. It is one thing for an individual to enjoy the fruits of Wisdom—but a much greater happening when he can share these unselfishly with all (Note 2).

"Know this: When the two flowers of the heart are fed and sleep; when the three flowers of the head are fed and go inwards; and the middle sentinel remains silent; then doth the dawn of consciousness, which is Cosmic, break and you become at one with—That which Is."

The heart centre consists of two Chakras or vortices of Power (See Plate 1). When these are fired by the Kundalini entering them, they blossom into full bloom and amalgamate together into one main Chakra through which forces may be taken into the Higher Consciousness from the outside; also through which forces from the Higher Consciousness may be radiated outwards. At this stage many elevated psychic manifestations are experienced. When Kundalini is risen above the heart, this Chakra is inhibited, because "She" also takes the whole of the Powers from the heart Chakra with Her in the ascent.

In the head there are three psychic centres. When the Power of Kundalini is risen to the Christ Centre, the secret centre below it is naturally inhibited, because all forces from that too have been risen upwards and the Christ Chakra becomes extremely active, operating as an all-seeing "Eye" and all-hearing "ear," so to speak. When these Powers are also risen by the Adept, on the vehicle of Kundalini, the culmination of this journey is the Crown Chakra. When this movement takes place, the Christ Centre or "middle sentinel," remains silent, or in other words, because of the inhibition of this centre, all basic thought as such, stops. The Adept is no longer able to detect outside stimuli through any one of the five lower senses. Thus he is in a physical state very near to death. The blood is protected from congealing and rigor mortis is allayed by a thin band of warmth around the head. In this state, all the inherent Powers of the Adept are lodged in the Crown Chakra and Cosmic Consciousness takes place (Note 3).

"Transmute limitation in the four fires and enjoy the light of the Fifth."

Which means, practise the Four Freedoms diligently and the time must come, by Karmic Law, when the ardent student will experience The Fifth Freedom which is Cosmic Consciousness.

AUTHOR'S RECOMMENDATIONS

NOTE 1. Study and practise "The Seventh Blessing," contained in, *The Twelve Blessings.* This will give a deeper appreciation of the true greatness of the Logos of Earth and put the student in tune with Nature's finer forces.

NOTE 2. Practice of *The Twelve Blessings,* will enhance such realization and give the serious student a better ability to make the great sacrifice when called upon to do so.

NOTE 3. See the Metaphysical lesson *Significance And Development Of The Psychic Centres,* for further instruction.

The above books and lessons are obtainable from the publishers of *The Nine Freedoms.*

SPECIAL NOTE. As supplementary reading matter to Chapter 5, the book, *Cosmic Consciousness,* by Richard Maurice Bucke, M.D. (published by E. P. Dutton & Co., New York) may be of great interest to students. However, it should be stressed, that some of the experiences reported by Dr. Maurice Bucke as being states of Cosmic Consciousness were only flashes of psychic phenomena experienced as "dreams," or in states of projection. Nevertheless, this book should give the beginner some small idea of the types of experiences which eventually lead up to true Cosmic Consciousness.

CHAPTER 6

THE SIXTH FREEDOM WILL BE ASCENSION

SAINT GOO-LING

"I Bless this Prasad with Power vested in Me. I Bless all this Prasad as sacrifice to Brahma.

"Afterwards dispense to all in sacrifice to Brahma.

"Now, at this time, people in physical body will be used as channels for Power which will be sent out for benefit of America. Sit still and relax. Close eyes and just let Power flow through you. It will then be manipulated by Devic Realms for country of America for reasons I have previously given. In this way you will be doing essential Service for all your brothers.

"I go."

MARS SECTOR 6

"This is Mars Sector 6 reporting from Satellite No. 3, now in Magnetization Orbit—Terra, during Magnetization Period No. 1, present phase.

"The Sixth Freedom will be—ASCENSION.

"Freedom from rebirth is brought about by he who is ready, as a result of countless experiences, countless lessons well learned through these experiences. Such a one has manipulated his Karma so that it forms a pattern, which proves that he does not need to learn the basic lessons which can be afforded, by further birth upon Terra.

"When this stage has been reached, the Adept then leaves this Planet Terra, through death, into a fuller life. Such a one may then choose whether or not he will remain upon Terra in order to render Service, or whether he will go onward to an introduction into the experience cycle of another Planet. At this stage, those with certain definite abilities volunteer to forego the greater bliss of an introduction into the experience cycle of another Planet and choose to remain upon Terra. A special Initiation is then afforded to the Adept who chooses to remain upon Terra and he is then Initiated into The Great White Brotherhood.

"ASCENSION is that Freedom which allows those of merit to perform greater Service.

"This state is not brought about until the Adept can consciously induce the state of Cosmic Consciousness.

"This state is not the result of any one practice, but rather the result of a culmination of experiences from which the vital lessons have been wrested; experiences which have been demanded by a specific Karmic pattern.

"There are few who have undergone an Initiation into The Great White Brotherhood. There are many upon Terra who make such erroneous claims. These are fools, for they only limit themselves.

"Truth is an essential part of total terrestrial experience. Until Truth is learned, the Freedoms cannot be enjoyed. Truth is the foundation of the temple of Freedom.

"ASCENSION will not be brought about by even Service in any ten lives. If, suddenly, the dawn of humanitarianism breaks over an individual lifestream, that lifestream then has to work for many lives in Service, in Spiritual ways and all of them, before even Cosmic Consciousness is possible.

"After this stage of awareness has been mastered, then lives ensue before total experience has been gained. Even so, it is the birthright of every lifestream upon Terra to enjoy the highest form of Initiation upon Terra—ASCENSION.

"This elevated state of being is not outside of your grasp, but within it. You can reach inwards, contact the great Spark of everlasting Divinity there, manifest this inner Spark in your outer thought and action and so manipulate your Karmic pattern that the higher Meditative states of Samadhi can be mastered at will.

"Then you are approaching—ASCENSION. You are then truly climbing the ladder of Evolution, for you then become a virtual

Flame in the darkness.

"A Flame which knoweth its Source.

"A Flame which forever pointeth upwards to that Source.

"A Flame which gaineth energy from itself.

"A Flame all transmuting, all vibrant, all living, all light.

"A Flame which cannot be extinguished.

"A Flame which burneth brightly despite all environment, all pressing condition.

"Such a one as this has a great auric field around themselves for they have no aura. Such a one as this transmutes all energies onto those planes which can then be tapped and used by others less evolved, thereby helping all lifestreams upon Terra.

"This is ASCENSION. It is not the result of decree, Mantra, or any other mystic practice, but the result of all Spiritual experience culminated into one facet.

"ASCENSION is like a single faced jewel. It is pointed. It reflects light and radiates light—and yet, it is made up of all jewels.

"Indeed is this great state a destination which has to be attained by sustained effort. Yet it is lasting. It is the ladder which terrestrial man can use to climb from the pit of terrestrial rebirth, so that he may then, unhampered, begin to climb the mountain of Transmigration.

"Know this: when the two faces of the heart are blue and cold; when the one face of the throat is pink and cold; when the three faces in the head are violet and yellow and violet and cold; then cometh great awareness.

"When the Globe above this head shineth through the consciousness of the individual and the Power, as stated, is risen and lodged in that place, then cometh—ASCENSION. But not until this time.

"Even in many that you regard as Masters upon Terra, the Power is still warm in these places. Karma cannot smile upon this warmness.

"Meditate upon these things and much will be learned.

"Practise the Freedoms as given, nor shirk any, for these are the steps from the pit of rebirth.

"The top of the mountain is—ASCENSION. You can, all of you,

gain this summit.

"Some of you will be needed to climb into the pit again, you will volunteer. You will do this and know everlasting greatness. Others will go on to other forms of Service.

"Indeed is ASCENSION a state of high elevation. It is not illusion, but as true as Truth.

"Take the Five Steps across the river of life and stand awhile, waiting on the Sixth—and you will know the Freedoms.

"The shortest distance which terrestrial man can take is the distance which is covered by the journey deep within; but it takes him longer to travel these relatively few millimeters than any other journey he will ever have to make.

"By perseverance, by Truth, by effort, by the radiation of Love, by Service in every form, he can make this journey and stand upon the rock of—ASCENSION.

"All Transmissions now discontinued."

Delivered on Sunday, March 5th, 1961.

ASCENSION

"Close eyes and just let Power flow through you. It will then be manipulated by Devic Realms for country of America for reasons I have previously given."

The reasons why the Power was sent through the audience invited to The Nine Freedoms, have already been given in Chapter 4, but the reference here made by Saint Goo-Ling that the Power was to be manipulated by the Devic Realms needs certain further explanation than that already given in Chapter 2.

During Metaphysical studies, you will see many references to the Devas, some of which will be difficult to understand unless you have at least some little idea of what the Devas are and what kind of Realms they inhabit.

The Devas are intelligences who inhabit physical bodies of a different type of matter than the gross material bodies of man. They live on the mento-physical Realms of existence which consist of the same type of etheric matter which constitutes their bodies. It is because of the difference in vibrations of this matter, that ordinary man is unable to see the Devas or to detect, with his basic five senses, the Realms they inhabit, even though these are exactly dovetailed into the physical planes of Earth. Now, just as physical men are inter-related one with another, so are the Devas inter-related upon their plane of existence. Just as physical man is existing in different stages of Evolution, so also are the Devas. Some of these are Enlightened Beings, who have even greater Power and Wisdom, in their own way, than any terrestrial Master. Some are more primitive and are commonly referred to as gnomes, elves and fairies which have been seen by clairvoyants and often by small children. There are even supposedly genuine photographs in existence of fairies.

The Devas are responsible for the manipulation of all primary and secondary energies upon the basic as well as higher planes. They are the Nature Spirits who, unlike man, work strictly according to Law. If you bring a flint into sharp contact with a wheel having a serrated edge, you will produce a spark containing heat. If you direct this spark on to a wick soaked with combustible fuel, you have a flame. According to Metaphysical Law, you have produced those conditions which are favorable for the invocation of and subsequent action of a Fire Deva. In this case the flame produced is a direct result of the manipulation of secondary or basic energy by the Devas. Had your wick been soaked with water you would not have been able to produce flame, or the conditions would have been unfavorable for the Deva to bring about the result determined by you.

If you pray and thereby release Spiritual energy on a psycho-Spiritual plane, this energy will eventually be manipulated by the Devas and if it is powerful enough to do what you wanted it to do, then this result will be brought about through the manipulation of the energy. If it is not powerful enough, then only a part of the result will be brought into being. If you send out negative thoughts, then the Devas will manipulate this energy and a negative type of result must come from the procedure. For instance, if everyone upon Earth possessed only an elevated thought and action pattern, thereby releasing the correct Power on to the etheric realms, one immediate result would be perfect weather conditions throughout the Earth. All violent storms would cease at once. There would be a perfect annual rainfall. The overall climate would become more temperate than it is now. Hurricanes, typhoons and similar destructive weather conditions would soon cease, because they are a result of the manipulation of energy by the Devic Kingdom, which has been transmitted to them by the violent expressions of emotion, hate, greed and similar negative discolourations put upon Universal mind radiated through man. These diverse reactions are the results of the manipulation of primary energy by the Devas.

We must all remember that between us and the Sun there is a giant natural battery which contains what the Ancients called—Prana, or what we might call—Universal Life Force. With every breath, every mouthful of food and every drink we take this Prana into ourselves, condition it and send it out again. Between you and the Sun there is also a whole Solar System full of what we might call—Universal Mind, which is taken in through the psychic centres, conditioned and transmitted out again. Now, Universal Mind is in a state of potential, or dormant state, until it has been conditioned by man. When it has, it becomes discoloured by his thought patterns. This discoloured mental energy must then be channeled, by Law, through the Devic Kingdoms, who must work according to inevitable Law. Action and reaction being opposite and equal, we must upon Earth reap the exact reaction to the thought patterns—discolouration of initial mind energy—which we possess. So therefore, it can be seen how important it is, not only to control the way we condition all energy absorbed, but to remember, that on another Realm exactly dovetailed into this one, there are workers of a tremendously high calibre, who will use this energy exactly as we sent it out to them for, to repeat, they work strictly according to the great Law of Karma (Note 1).

"The Sixth Freedom will be—ASCENSION."

"Freedom from rebirth is brought about by he who is ready, as a result of countless experiences—countless lessons well learned through these experiences."

As this Earth is a classroom, no man can leave it permanently until he has learned the necessary lessons which give to him the required qualifications to move on to a higher plane of existence. Reincarnation is, in the eyes of the great Masters, not a theory, but an essential part of Divine Truth, an aspect which, sooner or later, must be taught by every major Religion on Earth (Note 2). Not for very much longer can the orthodox leaders of the Christian Religion suppress the existence of Truth regarding reincarnation. The text tells us that, not only must we have countless experiences, but must learn well the lessons which these experiences have to teach before we can manipulate our Karma to such an extent that we prove that we are ready to leave the pit of continual rebirth into a physical body into this present cycle of existence.

"When this stage has been reached, the Adept then leaves this Planet Terra, through death into fuller life."

We will see in the following chapters what this fuller life really is and how it can be attained by all of us.

"A special Initiation is then accorded to the Adept who chooses to remain upon Terra and he is then Initiated into The Great White Brotherhood."

The Great White Brotherhood is a Spiritual Hierarchy, consisting of those advanced Beings, male and female, Who have undergone the elevated Initiation of Ascension and Who work in many ways from Their Retreats in various parts of the world. The Initiation mentioned in the text, refers to an actual Initiation of Ascension which is given to an Adept who chooses to remain on Earth in order to work directly for The Great White Brotherhood.

A graphic, eye-witness account of such an Initiation appears at the end of this chapter. This report is unique in as much as it is the first of its kind ever to appear in print in the whole of Metaphysical history. The author believes that he was granted the privilege of such an experience so that the connection between the Cosmic Hierarchy and this Earth could be shown, once and for all, in intimate detail. A close study of this happening will give the student some idea of the glory and magnificence of Ascension.

"This state is not brought about until the Adept can consciously induce the state of Cosmic Consciousness."

Ascension from this Earth has to be won. It is the culmination of all Spiritual thoughts and actions ever performed throughout the numerous lives of man upon this Earth plane. It is the end result of every experience he has ever undergone throughout his former lives and the essential lessons gained by those experiences, put into definite practice. When the text points out: "Until the Adept can consciously induce the state of Cosmic Consciousness," it means when the Adept can do this AT WILL. It is possible to have attained the elevated state of Cosmic Consciousness when all conditions have been exactly right and are virtually helping the Adept, to some degree, but this is not good enough and will not assure the next Initiatory step, which is Ascension. The Adept must be able to bring on Cosmic Consciousness, consciously and at will, whether conditions are helpful to him or not. This is where so many Metaphysical students fall short in their ideas. They believe that once an elevated state has been reached, it is no longer necessary to have complete Mastery over all conditions appertaining to that state, in order to be able to precipitate the same condition whenever desired. All students are informed, that, to achieve even a basic Meditative state once, is far easier than to attain this same condition at will when even astrological and other conditions may be against the attainment of such a completely disciplined state. The same applies, even more so, to Cosmic Consciousness. Therefore, it should be remembered that the Adept must be able to gain Cosmic Consciousness whenever he chooses, despite detrimental conditions which may exist at the time, before he can progress to the next step. This is a very different thing from being able to attain the state only once in a lifetime, as you will agree.

"There are few who have undergone an Initiation into The Great White Brotherhood. There are many upon Terra who make such erroneous claims. These are fools, for they only limit themselves."

This passage is self-explanatory, but its repetition here is necessary in order to help all readers to gain further powers of discernment and discrimination lest they be easily led astray by the false claims of others who obviously have not the knowledge and experience to back up such claims. Read again the pointers on discrimination given in Chapter 4 and other recommended literature if in any doubt whatsoever (Note 3).

"Until Truth is learned, the Freedoms cannot be enjoyed."

Complete and absolute Truth is essential in all your thought, throughout your daily lives, in all your meetings and business with others. Untruth has never, neither will it ever, bring to the seeker Truth. Before the seeker can ever discover Truth, he must, at all costs, be prepared to think and speak Truth himself. This is one of the essential steps upon the ladder of Evolution. There is no way around this step. Untruth, no matter how small, in your daily life will tend to repel Truth away from you. This must be remembered and strictly adhered to if you wish to realize your highest Spiritual ambitions. Speak truthfully and your search for Truth will be rewarding and, when found, it must be preserved with the greatest possible care.

"ASCENSION will not be brought about by Service in any ten lives. If, suddenly, the dawn of humanitarianism breaks over an individual lifestream, that lifestream then has to work for many lives in Service, in Spiritual ways and all of them, before even Cosmic Consciousness is possible."

This is a definite statement and it gives to you some idea of the loftiness of the state of Cosmic Consciousness, never mind Ascension which follows. Before even Cosmic Consciousness can be attained, you have to work for many lives in Service. This does not only mean to give Service, kindliness, help and guidance to your relatives, but to all people who need it, whether you agree with them or not, whether you like them or not, whether you consider them to be your friend or foe, you must pray for them continually, send your Love to them continually, give them Healing whenever they need it. Spend night after night of your life in Prayer for the world as a whole, drawing down the great tides of Spiritual energy which flow through the Cosmic System, conditioning these by your own pure thoughts and sending this energy out again, so that it can be manipulated by the Devic Kingdom on behalf of suffering, ignorant mankind. You must be prepared to continue giving, not only of your physical all, but your very life if necessary, to mankind. All this before even Cosmic Consciousness is experienced.

When Mars Sector 6 states: *"ASCENSION will not be brought about by Service in any ten lives,"* He means that you must begin, at once, to devote your life in Service to others. You can do this better through an organization of your choice, run by people with the right knowledge who know how to guide you into the realms of Service, or, if you choose, you can do this alone even though it is more difficult for you. It is believed that, should you start in Service alone, sooner or later you will want to join up with others who are engaged in an active form of Spiritual Service. It is a known fact, that when a few devoted students gather together and perform some Metaphysical practice, their cumulative Power is much stronger than it would have been if those same students had been separated.

You saw in Chapter 4 a remarkable proof of this statement. Those people who came together in different parts of America and Europe during the delivery of The Nine Freedoms, which was also a Special Power Manipulation, were used so effectively as channels for transmuting Power, that a devastating earthquake was arrested. It is a fact, of course, that the terrestrial cooperators could not have accomplished this outstanding feat had not certain Cosmic Masters seen fit to carry out the manipulations necessary for its accomplishment. But it should also be remembered that the Karma of mankind today is such, that a direct intervention of this nature by the Solar Hierarchy can only be allowed when it is made through human agencies. Therefore, although the manipulations were actually performed by Cosmic Intelligences, They would not have been allowed, by Karmic Law, to either stop altogether or arrest for the time being this earthquake, unless a sufficient number of dedicated people had proved their willingness to cooperate as channels through whom Spiritual Power could be radiated. Nothing of any note can be accomplished for the betterment of the world as a whole without the expenditure of considerable effort. Had the people who made up the cooperating groups during The Nine Freedoms not expended the effort to come together to perform "The Twelve Blessings," and other Spiritual practices for the world, the story would have been very different than it is today.

Thousands of people in Los Angeles owe their very lives and the further enjoyment of their property to the great Being, Mars Sector 6, and the relative handful of Americans and Europeans who helped in this great Spiritual Operation! It is a fact that a few really dedicated humanitarians, working alone, can do much good for humanity. But bring these together in a common Spiritual purpose and they can save the world. By so uniting their mental and physical forces, such a band can cooperate with the Great Plan for world Peace and Enlightenment.

Through the performance of such devoted Service to all they can prove themselves ready for their unbroken journey through progression to Enlightenment, Cosmic Consciousness and later even the elevated state of Ascension, an Initiation which can only be won through merit.

"Even so, it is the birthright of every lifestream upon Terra to enjoy the highest form of Initiation upon Terra—ASCENSION."
This is the most hopeful statement ever made to you!
IT IS THE GREATEST, MOST WONDERFUL PROMISE EVER MADE IN THE ANNALS OF PHILOSOPHICAL HISTORY!

You are told plainly, distinctly, directly by a Master of Cosmic Status that Ascension is your birthright and sooner or later you will enjoy this elevated Initiation. It is up to you and you alone how long you will suffer your present limitation before you advance yourself sufficiently to be able to take this last examination, the passing of which will enable you to leave the reincarnatory cycle of Earth. If you have any doubts regarding the validity of the Master's wonderful promise then your Intuition will soon inform you that it is perfectly true. Once you know this to be so, you should be fired with a firmer Spiritual determination than you ever believed possible, so that not even death can keep you from striving for this elevated goal. That is, unless you are willing to run with the hypnotized tide of basic humanity, content to while away your time in vague materialistic amusements. If you are, and again the choice is yours, you will involve yourself and have to suffer life after life of further limitation.

The Cosmic promise is hereby given to you. If you are wise and really practical, you will begin now to make the finest investment possible to any man—the investment of good deeds in a Spiritual bank, the interest on which can be taken with you, even when you die. If you live this life correctly, after death, you will go to another plane where you can learn more Truth so that you can return again in environmental conditions which are more helpful to you than the present ones. So, you can progress in active, suffering, but most wonderful Spiritual Service to—Ascension—your immortal goal!

"Such a one as this has a great auric field around themselves, for they have no aura. Such a one as this transmutes all energies on to those planes which can then be tapped and used by others less evolved, thereby helping all lifestreams upon Terra."

Those who have passed through the Initiation of Ascension have learned to take even the energies of their aura deep within "themselves," or their respective subtle bodies so that they can use and manipulate these subtle energies. Even though they have no auric field as such, their magnetic influence stretches for miles around. Wherever they go, they leave that place the better for their presence. Whoever they speak to is lifted in some way by their very words. For they have transmuted all the energies in such a way that they can be used by others who, either consciously or unconsciously, need strength, guidance and Life Force.

"It is not the result of decree, Mantra, or any other mystic practice, but the result of all Spiritual experience culminated into one facet."

Some uninformed mystical schools teach, that by the continual practice of their system of exercises, you can gain Ascension in this life. The text states quite definitely that this is not so. A thinking student does not need to be told that. If Ascension is as elevated as it undoubtedly is, then it is only obvious to all right thinking, discriminating people that not any one or even ten practices can guarantee to bring this state about. It must be the culmination of all Spiritual practices.

Ascension is the last step you take away from this Earth. How can you qualify to take this last step by only a few Metaphysical exercises? You cannot do so, no matter what those exercises are, or no matter who gives them. All any set of exercises can do, is to teach you how to discipline yourself and gain a greater Power so that, by the continual disciplined use of this Power, you may attain concentration, contemplation, Meditation and later Cosmic Consciousness at will, so that you may qualify for an even higher Initiation. No one practice or system can ever guarantee to give this to you, no matter who has invented it. Neither can the adherence to any single religious philosophy or thought qualify you for this last Initiation on Earth. To make yourself ready for this, you must have a workable knowledge of all philosophy, of all religious thought and this the most important fact of all, you must LIVE your religious beliefs and philosophies.

YOU SHOULD LIVE IN SERVICE SO ARDENTLY THAT YOU DIE IN SERVICE. If there is a key to Ascension, then that is it.

"Know this: when the two faces of the heart are blue and cold; when the one face of the throat is pink and cold; when the three faces in the head are violet and yellow and violet and cold; then cometh great awareness. When the Globe above this head shineth through the consciousness of the individual and the Power, as stated, is risen and lodged in that place, then cometh—ASCENSION. But not until this time."

This is a graphic description of the rise of Kundalini leading to the deep Samadhic state of Meditation. You will notice that, according to the text, the Kundalini has been risen through the heart, throat and up to and controlled within the Christ Centre. At this stage, a very deep state of Samadhic Meditation is gained. When the Kundalini is lifted even further than the Christ Centre up into the Crown Chakra, which is graphically described in the text as *"The Globe above this head,"* Cosmic Consciousness takes place. When this condition can be brought about at will, the result is Ascension. It is interesting to note here that, *"The Globe above this head shineth through the Consciousness of the individual"* means that the Soul, or Supra-Consciousness is bathed in the pure Light of the Spirit. This is the technical description of a very deep Meditative state. When the Supra-Consciousness, approaches or moves down the beam of this pure Light of the unmanifested Spirit, then it is time for Cosmic Consciousness to take place. When it moves nearer to the Spirit still, then it is time for an Initiation into Ascension. It should also be noted that, as elevated as the Initiation of Ascension is, even so, the Supra-Consciousness, although moved towards the source of this Light of the Spirit, is only bathed within this Light and cannot, at this stage, come into direct contact with the Source Itself. Such a contact happens possibly at some later stage, which is so elevated as to be beyond our comprehension.

"Some of you will be needed to climb into the pit again, you will volunteer."

The text here refers to people of very specialized knowledge and abilities who will be needed to stay on this Earth. These will be Initiated into The Great White Brotherhood. Possibly, a very chosen few, will be needed to live among mankind so that they can guide and help, especially when the great Cosmic Initiation of Earth comes, as it will do so. This will be a period during which the "wheat will be sorted from the chaff" and the most important time in the whole history of Earth. Even at the moment, master moves are being designed on the Inner Planes in preparation for this great Cosmic event.

Exactly what roles the very chosen few referred to in the text will play is known to them only, but it can be appreciated how vitally important their presence on Earth will be (Note 4).

"The shortest distance which terrestrial man can take is the distance which is covered by the journey deep within; but it takes him longer to travel these relatively few millimeters than any other journey he will ever have to make."

This is obviously true. It takes but a few hours to encircle the globe, a journey of at least 25,000 miles. But for man to travel the relatively short distance within, takes him countless lives. But it is interesting and indeed uplifting to note that this is the hardest journey he will ever have to make. When he goes to a higher plane of existence, after being able to make the journey within, towards Ascension, he will find himself well prepared to tackle the numerous problems he will have to solve on this higher plane of existence, or as Mars Sector 6 brilliantly describes it: *"A higher plane of Service."*

This is the crown you all can wear. It is up to each one whether or not you will reach out and accept your rightful position in the Cosmos, or whether you choose to continue in your present state of limitation. Remember always, that the Initiation of Ascension is the Metaphysical key which will unlock, forever, the gates to the pit of rebirth on Earth. Open this door and an unbounded field of Cosmic experience awaits you.

The finding of this mystical key is your birthright—step out boldly now and begin your search.

AUTHOR'S RECOMMENDATIONS

NOTE 1. It is strongly recommended that all students should make a careful study and regular practice of "The Fifth Blessing" contained in the book, *The Twelve Blessings.* Also recommended, *The Devic Kingdom*, which is a highly significant Metaphysical lesson which further explains the main function of the Devic Kingdom and its co-existence with mankind.

NOTE 2. Study, *Karma And Reincarnation,* for a clearer understanding of the working of this Divine Law.

NOTE 3. As an aid to the important ability to be able to discriminate between the true and the false teachers, the student should read, *My Contact With The Great White Brotherhood.* This book will also give you a deep insight into the hitherto mysterious workings of that Mystic Order and give you the location and inner workings of one of the most important Retreats on Earth—never before revealed to man.

NOTE 4. Read "The Initiation Of Earth," in *You Are Responsible!* (pages 145-159) for a complete statement by Higher Authority regarding this coming Cosmic Event. Also read "The New World," in *Cosmic Voice* Issue No. 23 (pages 23-26) and all the Transmissions in *Cosmic Voice* Issue No. 25.

All above lessons, magazines and books are obtainable from the publishers of *The Nine Freedoms*.

THE GLORY OF ASCENSION

The dimly lighted, gray paving stones beneath my hurrying feet seemed to drift into unreal oblivion as I made my way as quickly as possible towards my small apartment in London's teeming West End. The garish, cold, blue fluorescent streetlamps became significant markers of my progress. It was 7 o'clock on Friday, March 23rd in the year 1956. Just another day in the lives of the majority of people in the bulging metropolis, but to me, an important day, a day of promise— of great adventure.

Just previous to this I had been extended, what was to me, an outstanding invitation to visit the Third Satellite, which was then in orbit of Earth. The full impact of the honour bestowed upon me by this invitation grew, as I recalled that this Satellite comes into orbit of Earth at regular intervals in order to perform the outstanding task of radiating great waves of conditioned and concentrated Pranic energies to all Spiritual workers in the world. It was already known that the Controller of this gigantic Spacecraft was that outstanding Martian Adept, known simply to Earth as Mars Sector 6; a Cosmic Adept Who works directly under the guidance of the Lords of Karma.

As I hurried down that London street towards my little apartment, I was filled with some misgiving. Shortly, if all went well, I would be walking on most holy ground in the presence of Beings, Who were indeed great and I felt unprepared to meet Them. My feelings were not made any better because this had been a day of frustration. What could have gone wrong in my daily work, had done so. Instead of being able to leave my place of business in the early afternoon, I had been bound by delay after frustrating delay and now, with each step I took, the precious seconds ticked away. I knew that in order to prepare myself for a visit to this great Spacecraft, I needed several hours of intensive Yoga practice. Some of this precious time had already been lost. I would rather have lost drops of my own blood than wasted my time by business delays which were not important to me.

It seemed to take me twice as long this time to reach my apartment than it had done before, but eventually I arrived and somehow managed to steady my hand sufficiently to insert the key in the lock, open the door, pass through, close it and shut out the noisy city and its materialistic affairs.

As food seemed unimportant to me then, I bathed with great care, chose a chair in which I had meditated many times before and sat down facing the east.

The noises of the traffic on the street below, at first, permeated my thoughts. The frustrations of the day floated before me like some strangely animated pictures in what was to me then, a type of memory nightmare. I knew that detachment at this time was going to be difficult, but I also knew that the prize to me, was great, therefore, I set about my Yogic exercises with a grim determination. The small green light on top of a wardrobe cast a faint, almost sickly glow over the tiny, sparsely furnished room in which I lived. Somewhere below me there was a party going on. I could hear the laughter of a group of young people bent on a night's merriment. Regularly, what semblance of silence remained, would be raucously broken by some modern record badly played on a cheap reproducing instrument. But as I continued with my deep breathing, gradually the interfering sounds became more distant.

Slowly, but I was gratified to find, surely, the pale green light in the apartment became more remote. As I drew the breath in and locked it in the body, I felt the internal vibrations rise. Each breath was a step towards freedom, difficult, but sure. I continued with these exercises until I could detach myself completely from the noise of the party, the noises of the street and my surroundings. My breath became longer and slower. Then came the Sacred Mantra, over and over again, I repeated It. First with the eyes open, staring into the green light in order to gain the power of concentration. I took the balancing energies of this mid-spectrum vibration into myself through the eyes and gradually detached myself from the turmoil of my environment.

For some time I hovered in the mystic garden of peacefulness.

When I thought about the outside world a thousand different sounds rushed through my ears into my mind, and when I detached from it there was silence within. When I thought of that almost sickly green light, I could see the blues and reds in it and when I detached from it, it would fade into nothingness. Slowly, in mercy almost, my eyes were closed and I saw the lights within.

A thousand sparkling, different hued shapes floated before my inner vision. Beautiful some of them, incomprehensible others and yet, I detached my mind from them all and gently, environment slipped from my conscious awareness and I listened to the sounds within. I heard the great tolling, as of a distant bell, caused by the heart Chakra. The tremendous roar, as of giant rushing waters, caused by the forces revolving within the Christ Centre, seemed to blot out everything else momentarily from my consciousness. I concentrated so deeply upon this that the roar became deafening. It seemed that the room, the city, all the world should be aware of this great thunder as of a gigantic waterfall. At last, even this stilled to be followed by another sound. A rumbling note from outside of myself and yet, so much from within that its very presence seemed of the utmost intimacy to me. Like the sounding of a far-distant conch and yet from within me it seemed to come. This was the note of Creation—Itself. I recognized this as the all-pervasive Creative Sound of the Universe, the tremendous A-U-M, which is issued from the Lord of this Solar System, the Mighty Sun—Itself. At one time I was hovering within my body in deep Meditation, listening in supreme ecstatic bliss to the Creative Voice, and in the next moment, like a blinding flash—glorious freedom.

For a moment, I hovered there, within the room, regarding my pitiful body, now slumped forward in the chair, unbreathing, immobile, going cold. The next moment, I was above the city and in a twinkling, I hovered 1,550 miles in Space before a massive object.

From the outside the Third Satellite looks like an enormous egg. I made an estimation of its size to be at least a mile and a half long. Before me, around that floating Temple there was an impenetrable force screen. Yet, even as I neared the Satellite, I detected a movement within this screen. Forces seemed to whirl around and in the middle of the greenish glow of the screen an opening appeared which seemed like a bluish coloured tunnel through which I made my way. A door slid open and closed silently behind me.

I was inside the Third Satellite.

I became immediately aware that I was in a huge room, housing a tremendous amount of beautifully designed apparatus. The whole place was filled with a soft, exquisite radiance, more beautiful than that found in any place on Earth. The atmosphere was filled with an alluring perfume, not strong enough to be detected by the physical senses, but denotable by the reaction it had upon my etheric body. This perfume was an energy which, if concentrated upon, would bring on the deeper states of trance, regarded on Earth as Samadhi. Even though I did not really concentrate upon or tune into this perfume energy, its presence had a clearing effect upon my mind. In the middle of the ceiling, covering about a quarter of its huge domed surface, there was a large circular window. This was made of pure crystal, very finely ground and completely free from all flaws such as those which might be found in terrestrial glass, which would be likely to blur the images seen through it. The crystal window allowed the free passage of all Solar rays as well as magnetic rays coming from other Planetary Bodies, which latter shone against the purple background of Space with a scintillating brilliance never observed from the surface of Earth. The huge crystal window could be made into a filter by charging it with certain energies, affecting its selection of Solar and magnetic rays. During this charging process, the crystal changed colour from a soft rose pink, to a pulsating violet, according to the selection imposed by the Operators of the Satellite. Beneath the huge window stood three large crystal prisms which broke up the Solar spectrum into its primary colours. Each spectromatic colour was then split into seven further shades by another large crystal which held my fascinated gaze. This huge crystal structure seemed to be about 25 to 30 feet high, shaped like a giant egg. What its physical weight must have been, I do not know—but it defied all the known laws of gravity, because it floated in Space, being neither fastened to the domed ceiling or to the metal floor of the Spacecraft. Slowly revolving around this great egg-shaped crystal were numerous other multi-shaped crystalline formations. These moved in slow procession from the top to the bottom in an elliptical orbit. They passed between the tip of the ovoid and the great domed roof of the Spacecraft to continue their travel down the side of it, passing between the bright metal floor and the bottom of this gigantic egg. The great ovoid glowed as from some internal fires; obviously radiating energies which were conditioned by "something" within it.

The primary colours of the Solar rays, broken down by the three huge prisms, were absorbed into the ovoid structure and radiated outwards, each one split up again into seven further aspects of energy. These colours I could not name, because I have never seen their equivalent on Earth. But, I did notice, with great interest, that when each primary colour was broken down by the ovoid, the resultant energy seemed to flow slowly like a kind of liquid capable of being guided through the transmitting mechanism. The latter was made of a type of metal unknown to me, in the shape of a large matrix. This matrix was formed of intricate lines of metal which ran in very finely cut channels intersecting each other at exactly 90 degree angles. In fact, I was later informed that this angle of intersection was computed so exactly that the whole matrix had to be built in Space, so that the curvature of a Planetary mass would not affect the precise angles of intersection! From this matrix the conditioned energies were radiated to any destination on Earth.

The amazing scientists on the Third Satellite have, by a simple process of light manipulation, isolated the Universal Life Forces referred to by the Sages as—Prana. These subtle Pranas are the energies with which the Manipulators on the Third Satellite are flooding this dark little Planet during every "Magnetization Period." They can blend and interweave them in complicated patterns and guide the resultant energies to any spot on the surface of Earth.

I noticed immediately that all the crystals in the Third Satellite, unlike terrestrial jewels, seemed to glow from the inside—outwards. I learned later that these crystals were grown to an exact size and had a vibrational capability thousands of times that of normal terrestrial quartz.

I did not have the honour of meeting the great Cosmic Adept known as—Mars Sector 6, during this visit to the Third Satellite, but I did have the pleasure of meeting another great Master, Who answered all my mental questions. As I entered the huge Operations Room and looked about me, noting the mechanisms I have previously described, He approached.

He was a full seven feet tall with broad shoulders, narrow waist, and I noted quickly, abnormally small feet for a man of his stature. His skin was so suntanned, that it looked a glossy cinnamon colour. He wore a one piece suit, tight from the neck to the ankles. I did not see any seam or pocket or even a fold in that suit. It seemed to fit Him as though it had been poured around Him. In fact, rather than a suit, it seemed to be some type of force screen, although, as I reflect back now, I still believe that it was a solid garment of some kind. He looked about 30 years of age, but I learned later that He was at least 10 times that age. His eyes were dark and deep. His long brown, silken hair hung down to his broad shoulders. For a moment I caught His eyes and saw in them the depths of Wisdom I have never seen in any terrestrial eyes. As I was present in a projected state, I would have been completely invisible to an ordinary earthling, but He saw me easily and also could read my every thought. I noticed that His garment reflected the shades of the many hues of light playing on it, giving it a type of silvery sheen. When He moved, He did do with a controlled grace of a large cat. He gave me the impression of great physical strength and keen mental alertness.

As I had spent an average of eight hours a day for the past 10 years in the practice of Yoga which entailed a close study of the existence and natural flow of Prana, the first question that I wanted to ask was an obvious one.

"If," I telepathed, "these great energies flow through Space naturally, then why are you intensifying the activity at this time?"

The Martian smiled and when He did so, His dark deep eyes lit up with a light of complete understanding. He moved over to a rectangular shaped control panel, above which a large screen glowed dully. There was no noise as He manipulated several dials upon a panel before Him, but a picture of a Planet sprang on to the screen in vivid colours.

"Terra, like an habitual drunkard, is insensible to subtle stimulus," stated the Martian soberly. His beautiful choice of words cut right down to the heart of the problem, making long explanations not only unnecessary, but superfluous.

"That is Earth. Please notice the activity in the ionisation-belts."

I could see part of Earth glowing below very brightly on one side, gradually being shaded off on the dark side, which was turned away from the Sun. As other dials were adjusted, the projection of the mass of Earth itself was reduced to a dim background almost blotted out by a sea of violently agitated sparks, which buffeted against one another, splitting each other into smaller particles, in turn entering the nucleus of other atoms, causing minute explosions. Thus, was the chain ever going on—from molecule to atom throughout the whole great belt surrounding Earth.

"That activity is magnified thirty million times so that you can see it easily," went on my Martian instructor.

"With such activity as that, forming a barrier to the influx of the more subtle energies, you can understand the motive which prompts our activities here. The basic action of the ionospheric belts has been intensified by radioactive release within these units—which act as natural filters to break down Cosmic rays bombarding Earth. This intensification of 'ionic-flux' interacts upon Cosmic and Solar-rays in such a way as to reflect too much of their energy away from Earth—

hence the need for terrestrial bombardment from this Sector. Now, watch carefully...."

The picture on the screen changed and the whole world seemed to be rushing towards us at fantastic speed. So intently had I been observing the screen, that my mind was now captured by this latest development, causing every fibre of my etheric being to thrill to the apparent speed at which we were travelling. Actually, we had not moved from our orbit, the picture was the thing which changed as the focal length of the telescopic apparatus was lengthened to make the Planet appear to be nearer.

Europe, the British Isles, England, Middlesex, London... Mayfair, a street in Mayfair—and a solitary man staggering along under the lamps of that street, came into view! This living image materialized on the screen with such startling suddenness, that I gasped in amazement. From over 1,500 miles away, the wonderful Martian had been able to narrow down the field of vision to one single person in one single street. I could even see his rugged features plainly. The black bow tie around his neck was not straight—the silk faced lapels on his evening dress were crumpled...! As though this was not feat enough, the Martian continued to perform wonders with the dials until the terrestrial's aura came into view.

"That man is intoxicated," stated the Martian.

I could see the murky, thick, grayish aura surrounding the inebriate as he staggered about the pavement. I caught his jumbled thought pattern and recoiled at its revolting content.

Still in mental language, the Martian observed with a smile: "Not too good, is it? Now, such a man as that is becoming impervious to the higher aspects of mind, for he has taken within himself an alcoholic substance which is virtually causing an auric ossification. His aura is so clogged as to reflect away the more subtle, outside energetic-stimuli.

"The ionisation-units of Earth are becoming ossified rather like that man's aura. As alcohol acts upon that human aura, so radio-activity reacts upon the auric envelope of Earth, in a different way perhaps, but the results are similar causing a coarsening or ossification of a very finely-spun web and obstructing the passage of Nature's finer forces. Therefore, we have to intensify this existing magnetic flow, the intensity being predetermined by the terrestrial ability to absorb and use these energies. Look here."

The Martian began to manipulate switches and buttons on an oblong-shaped panel. As he did so, his long brown sensitive fingers moved rapidly from bank to bank, with the adeptship of a master organist playing a complicated tune upon a large magnificent instrument. Two more screens, one on each side of the main screen, came into glowing life. Upon one, I could see a complicated network of tiny glowing white dots, against a sea-green background. The other one was filled by a series of delicate colours, which seemed to come in at one end of the screen and travel along it to fade out on the other side nearest to the large middle screen, which latter was still filled by the picture of the drunken terrestrial. These different colours indicated energies being directed towards the man in the picture, but they were being reflected by his thick grayish cloggy aura.

"These bombarding energies are of a high vibratory nature and you will clearly notice how they are reflected away from our inebriated friend down there," informed the Master with a somewhat sad expression, momentarily clouding his beautiful countenance.

He turned aside from me and looked towards another Martian who was busy at the transmitting device. Although the other Martian had his back towards us, he turned immediately and looked across. The two of them lapsed into silence for a short time, then my instructor smiled at his colleague and turned once more towards his complicated looking panel. Not one word had been spoken, yet I knew that information had been passed between these two. I could see the subtle interplay of energies in their auric bodies as they regarded each other. Words were unnecessary for Adepts accustomed to communication by simple thought transference.

"You are in for a treat tonight!"

The words seemed now to float into my mind quite easily as the Master thought them.

"A girl from Earth has reached the stage of Spiritual evolution, which entitles her to an Initiation here. A Beloved Master from Venus is soon to join us and will perform the ceremony. We are always happy when such an event occurs, because we are privileged to be able to help another of our Earth-friends towards the Realms of the simple realization of Oneness. For indeed has another Flame, burning in the devoted heart of a dedicated Being, reached the desired intensity once more on Earth, and the Lords of Karma have granted us the energy necessary to fan this Flame into the pure Light of Ascension."

I lapsed into a deep, sad silence, as I thought about the millions of my fellow earthmen who, like the drunkard on the screen, were building barriers for themselves against such marvelous Holy Powers. That very moment, even as I stood there, they were doing this. Even as I stood—in that virtual floating Temple of God—great natural energies from the Sun and the other Planets were being reflected away into purple Space by the barriers which men had built around their green Earth, by their absurd use and experimentation with powerful radioactive forces of which they knew little or nothing. Why should they ever be forgiven for such wanton vandalism? How could a small handful of right-thinking, right-living men and women tell these things to the unlistening masses?

And when they tried to do so, what other result than sarcastic jeers of disbelief?

"But today's sarcastic jeers can turn into tomorrow's joyous cheers."

The Master's simple faith assured me. He was by my side, charging my mental aura with optimism and confidence, strengthened by His vast experience.

"Come," invited my tall Martian instructor, leading the way from the banks of dials in the control panels, towards what appeared to be a smooth grey wall. When He was a short distance from the wall, a section moved briskly and silently into the floor, revealing a corridor beyond.

"You will undergo certain experiences," He explained.

"Do not be afraid, these feelings will be the result of manipulations calculated to prepare your mental bodies in some degree for what you are about to witness."

This statement floated into my mind as I followed the Martian into the corridor. Hardly had we crossed the threshold, before the door slid back into place behind us and at the same time the narrow corridor became flooded with a bright orange coloured light. It seemed to radiate from the floor, walls and ceiling, all at the same time. I felt a mild shock at first, but this was followed by a surge of Power which caused me to grit my mental teeth in an effort to control a new found exuberance. I seemed to hear or feel a deep booming sound in the distance as though it came from thousands of miles away. Immediately, I became aware of, in fact I could actually see, my own physical body fifteen hundred miles away, sitting in deep trance back on Earth. A quick look around told me that the Martian had disappeared, but I was not at all worried by this.

The colour radiations changed slowly towards yellow. When a liquid golden hued yellow vibration predominated, I felt quite suddenly very old, very old indeed, as though the years on Earth had been nothing save a passing moment in the experience of total existence. Memories, stripped clear of the lock of forgetfulness, came surging upwards like an avalanche. Pictures began to form in my mind and I could think and describe these scenes in a strange tongue which was certainly unlike English. I knew then how limited language was as a means of thought expression. It was but the result of the resistance caused by the thinking processes through the different brain centres which slowed down the thought vibrations, so that they could be comprehended by the conscious part of the Earth mind and, therefore, limited true translation in accordance with common conscious understanding.

The booming sound became louder and slightly lower in tone. Gradually, gently, almost subtly at first, the yellow radiance gave way to green. This energy brought with it different reactions, for I now became very steady in my thinking. As each thought came to me, I wanted to analyse it carefully before expressing a mental opinion, to handle it in my mind, as it were, to feel the very core of its construction before acceptance or rejection.

The deep booming note continued, but now on the top of it came a very high pitched whine. The radiance changed into the higher vibratory rates, the blues of the spectrum became predominant and I became aware of a new phenomenon. It seemed as though, by some magical means beyond my comprehension, a wind had quickly sprung into being, a wind which increased in strength until it became a veritable gale. But the amazing thing was, I now moved faster along the corridor, despite the fact I was advancing in the teeth of such a mighty hurricane, that had my physical body been there, the cellular structure would have been destroyed by friction.

The blue radiance became so intense and the vibrations so fast and short that, had it not been for this hurricane now raging through my subtle body, I would have suffered some kind of etheric lesion caused by temperatures which must have been unbelievably low. Further back went my memory during the blue radiance, back into the ancient depths before time existed as a dimension of limitation. Things were seen and felt which could not now, nor ever be expressed in words. But one great Truth stood out more gloriously than it ever had done before in my consciousness. This dominating Truth was a revelation—old but ever new. In the Beginning, All was Spirit—and that Spirit was Divine.

One last vivid, violet-coloured flash and it was all over. I was out of what I had thought was a corridor and found myself standing on a little balcony overlooking an amazing scene. The Martian Adept was there to greet me. His calm manner and gentle, almost feline grace, acted like a soothing balm, which eased away the shock caused by the scene below.

The room was as large as a moderate sized theatre, with a high ceiling. Around the walls hung many delicately coloured draperies one colour blending with its neighbour, denoting an artistic arrangement which was sheer delight to behold. From the high domed ceiling came a diffused blue light, which seemed to enhance the colour of each tapestry it touched by some strange magic, making them glow with a living radiance of their own. Nothing was dull and although not loud in any way, everything in the great hall seemed to live. The same delicate perfume which I had previously sensed, pervaded the whole atmosphere, bringing peaceful satisfaction when absorbed.

Towards one end, set upon a dais with long steps leading up to it, was a large straight-backed chair made of crystal, looking rather like a throne. The throne itself glowed with a soft rose pink radiance, making it appear like illuminated mother-of-pearl. On the right hand side of the throne was a tube some six feet high. Its diameter was large enough to accommodate an average-sized human in the standing position. On one side of this glassy looking tube, was a control panel beneath an oblong shaped viewing screen. There followed row upon row of low seats covered with the same materials as composed the draperies, and the varying colours again seemed alive in a quiet way. I could see from my little balcony, which was situated about half way along one side and a few feet higher than the rows of seats, that the splendid hall was now empty.

"This is the Assembly Room of the Ship," informed the Martian.

"This morning, for it is early morning where you dwell, the Room will be used for a very special purpose. It is desired that you speak of the things you are about to see here, so that those who are open-minded may have a preview of the glories which await them."

"But Sir," I interrupted, "I could never write in words alone a worthy description of this Room, far less that which you say is to come."

The Martian smiled gently and extended his right arm towards me with the fingers together and pointing upwards with the palm facing me.

"The best you can give when you arrive back on Earth, my son, will suffice. You see, if you describe this happening in your own words, it will be understood. These words will be simplified by Truth as you see it and in the same way as you see it, so also other men will see it."

Despite his kindness, dear readers, I feel that I should make it known at this juncture, that to do complete justice to what happened is beyond the limited capabilities of an ordinary man like myself. Therefore, I trust you will all bear with me and regard my limitations with due tolerance.

Any further comments concerning my shortcomings were cut short, because the cream and green draperies on the wall opposite the throne began to rise slowly. There was no noise as this happened. A large arch was revealed through which people began to enter the hall.

I was struck by the gay colours they wore. The ladies were dressed in long garments, taken in at the waist by jewelled bands which scintillated in the living glow from the ceiling. Their dresses seemed to be made of a kind of satin velvet which changed its hues as they moved with a wondrous grace, which caused me to gasp mentally. The ladies garments reached almost to the floor, but from my position I could not see what kind of shoes they wore.

The men wore loose fitting multi-coloured garments rather like silk blouses and wide trousers drawn in around the waist and ankles. Some had loose sleeves and some were gathered together in such a way as to cause the folds of material to take on a varying-coloured sheen in the light.

To see this handsome and very colourful assembly and to know the reason for their coming here, gave me a mental jolt. If such a gay, colourful dress were worn at an Earth meeting for a solemn Religious service, it would be frowned upon, to say the least. But there was nothing solemn or sanctimonious about this gathering.

"Why should there be?" broke in the Martian, reading my thoughts.

"Some terrestrial Religions separate happiness from the worship of God. Surely, if you believe in a Divine Creator, then such a belief in itself and all that it means, should be a source of never ending joy.

These people are from many different Planets, some from outside of this Solar System, but there the main difference ends, for they are united in their joyousness because this girl from India has risen to such heights. They have come here to help in the Initiation and to rejoice because of their ability to help. Every member of this Assembly has already undergone this Initiation into the glorious realms of Ascension, even as did the person you call Jesus Christ."

The silence was broken by strains of music coming from some hidden source. A wonderfully blended rhythm seemed to come from all places at once and to fill every part of the great hall with an equal intensity of sound.

I detached my thoughts from the physical structures of the people in the Assembly Room for a short time and looked at their etheric bodies. Oh, what a marvellous sight!

There must have been about four or five hundred individuals in that hall, yet they were so much in loving harmony with one another, that their etheric bodies seemed to blend and form one single united aura. So united were they by a common expression of Spiritual devotion to one another, that I saw them as parts of one amalgamated lifestream. I quickly checked my mind which recalled the picture of a similar meeting of terrestrial people, which revealed the motley of etheric and mental barriers and jealousies which turned their subtle bodies into a murky reddish, grey flecked mass. I shuddered at the comparison.

With one accord, the Assembly raised their clear voices in a song of praise. The words were not in English, they had a musical sing-song quality more like Chinese than any western language. The singing and the tones of the music blended together with perfect unison, as though the two parts of the sound had become dovetailed into one complete whole. A melody which was beautiful beyond description filled the Assembly Room so completely, that it echoed and re-echoed in lilting whispers even after the music ceased. It seemed that, once created, the song and music assumed a form of its own, a life given to it by the breath of those majestic creators.

The chorus stopped and through a small doorway on the left of the throne came the Indian girl, led by several beautifully clad, elegant ladies. The Earth girl wore a single white robe which reached to the floor. She looked the picture of happiness and grace. As she glanced towards the throne, her dark eyes shone, but on her face there was an expression of joyous peace. I could see immediately that, although she was only about eighteen years old, in this incarnation, here was a very advanced Being who, with her kind and gentle calmness, became a veritable Spiritual giant in comparison with the likes of myself.

Both she and the whole Assembly must have picked up my thoughts, for with one accord they looked in my direction, smiling happily as they did so. Had I been on Earth in my present state, I would have been invisible, yet all these people could easily see me and fully understand my thought pattern.

Now, a complete silence settled over the whole Assembly. I gazed intently, feeling a ripple of earnest anticipation from those people from other Planets. They all stood immobile, not a fidget or whisper save the subtle lingering impression of the music. Even this seemed to cease, leaving a silence so complete that it could be felt like a living thing. I had previous knowledge of this Silence, but, even so, was just as impressed then as I was during the first experience of it. I knew that a Great Presence was there and I did not have long to wait before this was confirmed.

There came three parallel lines of purple fire which crossed the huge domed ceiling from end to end. Then a brilliant white "cloud" entered through the roof itself and floated gently down to the dais. There was a whirl of colours within this glowing cloud and slowly and steadily before our very eyes, a human form resolved itself to stand in all its Glory upon the dais.

The Master from Venus had arrived.

He looked ageless, appearing neither old nor young. He was very tall, straight and slim, with long golden hair which hung down to his straight, broad shoulders. Like the locks of some fastidious woman, His hair shone like burnished gold. Gently tinted by the reflection of the blue radiance from the roof, it seemed majestically alive. The blue flickers of light, dancing over those locks of streaming gold like some fairy "will-o'-the-wisp," seemed to caress it with light fingers of magic fire.

He was attired in a simple robe of white, drawn in around His slim waist by a broad band which sparkled with the light from a complicated pattern of multi-hued jewels. These jewels were really crystals which had different rates of vibration, according to their colour and composition. Like the crystals in the Operation Room of the Satellite, these also seemed to glow with a radiance of their own.

"That band is not an adornment," informed my Martian instructor.

"It is a mark of status and is indeed, as you have already noted, a sceptre of Power which is carefully balanced and perfectly attuned to the vibrational capabilities of the wearer."

"You mean," I inquired: "That the belt of crystals is attuned to the wave-length of the Master and if anyone else wore it they could not use it?"

"That is correct," He answered.

"If anyone, who had not undergone His stages of Initiation, were to wear it, its function would be reduced to that of some handsome-looking trinket which they could not energize. That band can be activated by Him when He wishes to use the vibrational pattern of those crystals as a focal point of concentration so as to bring into physical manifestation His thought forms."

I gasped as the implication of this statement gradually became apparent to me.

"Could you tell the name of this—this Angel?" stammered I.

The great man from Mars smiled in kindly tolerance.

"We seldom, if ever, give names and there is a good reason for it. However, such a One as this, may be called a 'Kumara' on Terra.

"In fact," he went on slowly, with a twinkle in his eyes: "He has been known by many names on Earth. Some ancient and even modern sages refer to Him as, 'The Tall Master from Venus; for He has visited there many times and has even landed on Earth many times."

"Then there is truth in the stories about a Saint with golden hair, occasionally seen by the Yogis of India and Thibet?"

"Some are true," answered the Martian quickly and with, or so it seemed, finality. I did not press this question any further.

I waited to see the Master from Venus take His place on the throne, but I should have known better, for One of such calibre needs no throne. Instead, the young Indian girl was led with gentle and loving care up to the great crystal chair, where she sat down. The lady attendants then took her small brown hands and crossed her wrists, laying her right palm over her heart and the left on the opposite side of her breast. Her large eyes never left the majestic, tall and radiant figure of the Master, whose beneficent countenance was lit up by a wonderful smile. Even from where I stood, I could see His blue eyes—blue, like a cloudless summer sky, they held the depth of Space itself. He advanced, stretched out His right hand, placing His thumb lightly on the centre of the girl's forehead, extending His long fingers fanwise above her shining black hair.

No movement came from the gathering as He closed those wonderful eyes and slowly stretched His left arm sideways and upwards and then slowly downwards again towards His heart. I watched in fascination, rooted to the spot by the magnificence of it all. Slowly, that white-clad arm moved and that glowing left hand came nearer and nearer to the spot over His heart. The young girl had closed her eyes now, seeming to be in a state of ecstasy. The profound silence of Space itself settled over the whole Assembly. They were all standing, eyes closed, faces immobile, as though they were carved images.

Oh, dear readers, would that I could do this Sacred scene real justice, but alas, I cannot. Out of necessity and not choice, I must offer only a crude description to you here, for I know not common words that would do it justice. It was though Time stood still and the very axis of Life-Itself waited for He Who, in glorious radiance, now stood motionless with His right hand still over the slim girl's head and His left palm over His own heart.

The large band of crystal jewels around the Master's waist began to glow more brightly, until they looked like tiny suns. The throne too, began to gleam with an inner white fire which became brighter and brighter until it was so brilliant it dazzled even my etheric eyes. The Assembly of Planetary Beings were all gazing unflinchingly at this indescribably brilliant light. No terrestrial could have looked at it through physical eyes even for one second, for such was the dazzling intensity of the brilliance it would have blinded him instantly.

The girl's physical body gradually became more and more hazy and misty-looking. I could dimly see now right through it. Then came a deep blue flash of light from the base of the spine upwards. When this reached her head, a golden fire was lighted there. Her physical body melted away completely, until only her etheric remained. Then I gasped in genuine astonishment, for the Saint from Venus, with eyes still closed, raised His right hand slowly, palm facing the high crystalline tube on the right of the dais. A streak of purple fire from His outstretched palm brought the tube into glowing life. Flash upon flash of brilliant colours blended and intermingled in that tube, some in long straight lines, some in curves, waving like snakes as they curled about each other, winding and interwinding like live things. A bubbling, seething, living mass of ever moving colours filled that gigantic tube, making it look like a kaleidoscope of the very Gods Themselves.

Then came the music again, from out of the space around us, it seemed to ebb and flow like liquid as it penetrated the whole place with an equal intensity. There were no instruments visible, yet the music came, each note beautifully related to its neighbour as if they were cells in the body of a perfect rhythmic whole. Perfume filled the air, gentle and alluring. It seemed to come from nowhere and yet, from everywhere simultaneously, caressing the senses with a fragrant delicacy, it brought joy to my very Soul. With one accord, the whole Assembly broke into a triumphant song of Heavenly praise.

At that moment, the girl stepped out of the long thin tube and stood gloriously radiant before us all!

Every cell of her physical body had, during this ceremony, been broken down and then re-created—before our very eyes. She was still the same small fragile figure as before, but she now possessed a form which was beautiful to behold. Her calm, gentle expression, large kindly brown eyes and smooth olive skin, her long glistening black hair flowing over her shoulders and full-length white gown under which peeped her tiny feet clad in jewelled sandals, made a picture that was exquisite and a sheer delight to look upon. For that young girl, now in her Ascended Body, had the beauty of purity which is lasting. Now, that clean feminine beauty was agelessness itself. No ravages of cruel time would ever bring one wrinkle across that perfect symmetry.

"When the time for Revelation comes, my friend, Terra will recognize such Beings as she has now become, and will have cause to bless them. That girl could have left Terra forever, because she has now evolved above the necessity for experiences offered by that Planet. However, recognizing the dire need of Spiritual assistance to Earth, she decided to remain. Therefore, the Lords of Karma granted the energy required to give to that evolved Soul an ageless body. She will soon return again to poor Earth and work for what you would call the 'Forces of Light', as a member of that universal order—The Great White Brotherhood. Such a sacrifice is made gladly by that little girl," explained the Martian.

"Such a selfless sacrifice is the measure of Evolution," I answered.

I knew that in a short time, a young Indian girl—radiant in her youthful, yet wise simplicity—would be walking amongst us back here on Earth. No one, at first glance, would be able to pick her out from dozens of other lovely eastern girls. Yet there is one great difference, for unlike the majority of men and women on this Earth, she will never grow old. A thousand years will not bring a single grey hair, or a solitary wrinkle to that smooth brow. To her, belongs the lasting beauty of simple purity.

I blinked my physical eyes and gradually became aware of the dim green light, casting its radiance over the dim little apartment. My limbs were so stiff that they ached when I moved. I was perished with cold. Even so, somehow I managed to balance the Pranas within the psychic centres. Then moved around the room to bring the circulation back into my cold aching limbs.

When I had regained enough strength to do so, I threw back the window drapes and looked out, gazing at the dingy, unpainted houses across the street. It was 3 a.m. Most of the city slept after the useless toil of the previous day. I looked upwards—past the dull grey slate roofs of the houses—up into the huge clear sky. Way up there, somewhere in the immeasurable vastness of full Space, Great Beings were toiling ceaselessly for us all.

I recalled the picture of the drunken man in Mayfair and how his aura made so gross by his overindulgence, had repelled the energies of inspiration; the beauty of the eastern girl as she stepped, elegant and radiant from her Initiation of Ascension—the elusive yet strongly alluring perfume energy which permeated the vast Spacecraft—the colours—the giant crystals—the silence—the wonderful music which seemed to be a separate entity, yet was an essential part of Them all—the tall, cat-like grace, yet magnificent compassion of the Martian Who, with gentle patience had answered my blundering questions. I remembered vividly, the mighty work these Great Beings were doing for all men upon Earth—and the sadness They must, in compassion, feel when They looked down and saw man as he is, yet knowing and being able to compare this pitiful sight with man as he could be.

Despite myself, I was so overcome, that I wept aloud....

CHAPTER 7

THE SEVENTH FREEDOM WILL BE INTERPLANETARY EXISTENCE

SAINT GOO-LING

"By Power vested in Me, I Bless this Prasad in sacrifice to Brahma. I Bless all in sacrifice to Brahma.

"Afterwards dispense to all.

"Now, again during this time, you will be used as channels for energies which will be sent to the Devic Kingdom and from there dispensed over country of America for reasons previously stated. Relax and tune into flow of energy. Also, remember that in other countries, at this time, people are working to help you to help your country. Do not forget to send these your thoughts as well.

"I go."

MARS SECTOR 6

"This is Mars Sector 6 reporting from Satellite No. 3, now in Magnetization Orbit—Terra, during Magnetization Period No. 1, present phase.

"The Seventh Freedom will be—INTERPLANETARY EXISTENCE.

"After the Initiation of Ascension, the lifestream passes from Terra and either returns to work upon Terra, or goes to another classroom in the Solar System. In this case, the lifestream would be born on to another Planet through the Flame of the Logos of that Planet. It would not be born through the womb of the female, spending some time in a re-enactment of its evolutionary process as happens when a lifestream returns to Terra.

"In the case of Planetary birth upon a higher sphere of Evolution,

138

the lifestream, in its Ascended body, would be requested by a male and a female upon that particular Planet. It would then be born through the Flame of the Logos of that Planet, as an adult. Once introduced into that Planetary Scheme, it would retain its original body for many centuries. When it became necessary to change this body, it would break up the cellular structure and reform another cellular structure for itself.

"Freedom from terrestrial rebirth is indeed a great and decisive step made by the lifestream towards total existence. No longer is such a lifestream petty, prone to basic limitation, prone to like or dislike, as it was previously. The experience of Cosmic Consciousness, the experiences of Ascension, are indelibly stamped upon the Soul Principle of such a lifestream in such a manner that it tries with all available energy to express its Divinity.

"A Planetary birth in this way leads to a realization of the limitation imposed by the recognition of basic dimension and a will to overcome this imposition, this limitation—a will to forge through Interplanetary Service to even greater realization and appreciation of the whole unity of all things.

"The first Planetary step taken through Ascension from Terra will result in an introduction into either the Planet Mars, Neptune, Jupiter, or Pluto.

"The next step, which is the second part of this Freedom, results in an introduction into the Planet Venus or the Planet Uranus, where different experiences are gained.

"But note this: there is upon the way a stopping place. This may not be mentioned save to say that even though the Sun is dark, the energy is still felt. In that statement is a clue which does not, of course, intimate that the stopping place is a Sun.

"From there greater Freedom is realized. Interplanetary man is no longer bound to the clay of Terra or the clay of any other Planet. He is free to serve throughout the Galaxy—even outside of the Galaxy.

"A great and deep appreciation and realization of the totality of Divine existence lives within such a one. He does not pay lip service to anything existent, or non-existent, but begins to be a knower; begins to realize the 'why' of existence. Already he knows the 'how'—and so with his travel comes broadness. No longer is he even limited to a base physical structure, for he discovers that by excitation of the internal molecular working, he can form this base structure into finer matter which he can propel through full Space.

"He begins to study the smallest atom in Space—the greatest Sun in Space. He begins to work towards the perfect singular Vortex and the perfect Vacuum. He is capable of experience in more than one system of dimension at the same instant. Yet he is not limited by a time continuum as is terrestrial man. For Interplanetary man is above time, because he is part of it; not part of the result of change, as is terrestrial man, but a part of the change itself.

"As he goes deeper into this Freedom, he realizes his great Power as a ray capable of the manifestation of thought visualizations. He becomes a tiny thought Creator. He learns to control his visualizations so that they conform exactly to predetermined patterns.

"He learns the greatness of the Great. To him the Divine is reflected through his Masters upon Saturn. He would rather give up even his present Freedom and be cast into the lowest terrestrial astral realms, than disobey his Masters, by even a glance—by even a glance!

"He does not worship his Masters because of Their Power, but because They are a reflection of the Divine Principle.

"Such a one is many lives further along the road to Cosmic realization than even an Earth Master.

"Take the Five Steps. Wait upon the rock of the Sixth, so that you might experience—Ascension—and go forward and become Interplanetary man.

"Know this: the wheel turns twice and the red globe dispels the darkness, so that the yellow globe may rise. In the rising comes realization. When the blue globe intersects the yellow globe at the right angle—consciousness is born. When the green globe causes fusion between the two, realization of consciousness takes place and all the colours are manifest. When the violet globe rises into the Golden Sphere, the crescent of Wisdom is born and—shineth.

"This is the secret of—Creation.

"It is the secret of—Preservation.

"It is the secret of—Transmutation.

"It is the Sacred Word—A-U-M.

"You have been told. Guard well this Sacred Wisdom, for even though you understand it not—now, there will come a time when you will.

"Your internal vibrations have been altered by these utterances. Do not ever again slip from the path, for if you do, your fall will be doubly hard.

"Take this Cosmic Wisdom deep into your heart and a greater realization will dawn and when it does—and as it does—walk forward boldly into—The Seven Freedoms.

"I have spoken thus.

"All Transmissions now discontinued."

Delivered on Wednesday, March 8th, 1961.

INTERPLANETARY EXISTENCE

"Relax and tune into flow of energy. Also, remember that in other countries, at this time people are working to help you to help your country."

This instruction was given to attendees of The Nine Freedoms as a reminder that The Aetherius Society had set up a chain of cooperators throughout the world, many of whom belonged to religious denominations other than the Society, who were tuning into the energy released to the world and sending this out to help the country of America, exactly at the time that these Freedoms were being given. If you refer back to the beginning of the commentary on The Fourth Freedom, you will see why this was so necessary.

"The Seventh Freedom will be—INTERPLANETARY EXISTENCE."
"... or goes to another classroom in the Solar System."

This reference means to a higher plane of existence on another physical Planet in this present Solar System. As to which Planet that is, we will see later on in this text.

One important fact should be made clear at this point, to avoid any misunderstanding in the mind of the student. The vast majority of the Lifestreams now inhabiting the other Planets, referred to later in the text, have not needed to pass through the experiences offered by life on this Earth. The main reason for this is made clear in the Introduction to The Nine Freedoms. It is shown how man, now on Earth, had committed the base Cosmic crime by causing the death of the Planet, "Maldek." After such involution, he had to be restricted by gross limitation or, in other words, he had to learn the basic lessons which could only be experienced on this Earth. The Beings on other Planets, not marring their Evolution by such a terrible act, continued to progress on Their higher planes of existence.

As pointed out earlier, this accounts for the vast difference between Earth man and Interplanetary man. It also shows why the majority of Interplanetary people have not had to come down to the lowest classroom in the Solar System before They could rise up again. This has happened only to terrestrial man. After centuries of being kept ignorant as to his line of Cosmic progression, terrestrial man is now being informed, in this unique text, of his road through Evolution.

"It would not be born through the womb of the female, spending some time in the re-enactment of its evolutionary process as happens when a lifestream returns to Terra."

As we will learn later in the text, the propagation of the race through the womb of the female is a process only necessary to very backward life forms such as those found upon Earth. It is interesting to note that, in the course of its Evolution in the womb, the body of an incarnating terrestrial lifestream is first like a fish and then a hairy animal similar in many ways to a monkey, before it eventually takes on a human form, namely that of a baby.

The full implications of this process will be revealed to the student at the right time in Meditation. It should, however, be noted that life itself, while possessing only an intelligence potential is, under certain conditions, motivated by a memory faculty. This inherent memory faculty can cause the life energy to revert back to an original state, given the correct environmental conditions such as the womb of the terrestrial female.

The incoming will of the reincarnating human is capable of imposing that direction upon the basic life energy, through applied intelligence, which causes the life energy to be evolved up to the level upon which the consciousness intends to use it in order to gain experience. (See explanation of the seven dimensions of Creation later in Chapter 7.)

The text here is not stating that man, as we know him, evolved from a fish. Instead, it is reminding us by reference to a known biological fact, that life, during "birth" is then and always has been, expressed in numerous ways in order to help the expressing intelligence gain experience.

It should be remembered that life is a basic motivating force which is used by intelligence and directed by will in order that a predetermined pattern of Evolutionary progress can be accomplished (Note 1).

"In the case of Planetary birth upon a higher sphere of Evolution, the lifestream, in its Ascended body, would be requested by a male and a female upon that particular Planet."

When a lifestream is to be introduced into the reincarnatory system of another higher Planet in this Solar System, a male, or positive creative force and a female, or negative preservative force, is chosen to make a request for this Initiated lifestream, prior to its introduction on to that Planet. Needless to say, sex does not, in any way, enter into this introduction. There is no intimacy whatsoever between the male and female upon a more highly evolved Planet as there has to be on Earth in order to propagate the race.

"It would then be born through the Flame of the Logos of that Planet, as an adult."

After a strong mental request is made by the chosen guardians of the lifestream which is ready to come into the environmental conditions of a higher Planet, then, in its Ascended body, it actually enters the life cycle of that Planet as a full grown adult. This entry is made through the Flame of the Logos, or Life Force of the Planet Itself. This must be a very advanced type of mystic Initiation, the like of which no terrestrial has any knowledge.

"Once introduced into that Planetary scheme, it would then retain its original body for many centuries.

"When it became necessary to change this body, it would break up the cellular structure and reform another cellular structure for itself."

We have seen, during the Initiation of Ascension, how a relatively perfect physical body is made for the lifestream to inhabit. This original body is capable of living for hundreds of years. If, through age or cellular fatigue, or for any other reason unknown to us, some change has to be made in this physical body, it is not necessary for the body to become incapable of withholding life, in other words, die, before this change can be made. If a change is necessary, then the lifestream disengages itself from the physical envelope and consciously breaks up the cellular and possibly even the molecular structure of its physical vehicle and then builds for itself a finer, more usable body. After this advanced procedure, the lifestream enters the reconditioned physical structure which is capable of containing life for many more centuries (Note 2).

"The first Planetary step taken through Ascension from Terra will result in an introduction into either the Planet Mars, Neptune, Jupiter, or Pluto."

This is a very definite statement, although the text does not state the exact chronological order of progression through the Planetary classrooms. This possibly depends upon how best the abilities can be used in the great Cosmic Scheme of Evolution. The text does infer though, that the evolving intelligence may have to visit each of these Planets in order to gain experience, to render the necessary Service and possibly interchange between Planet and Planet as experience becomes wider, awareness deeper and ability so pronounced that it can be used to its best advantage upon different experience levels. It must be remembered that the intelligence entering the environmental conditions of Mars for the first time, even though it is an adult in an Ascended body, would feel rather like a newly born baby entering life on Earth. The culture of this Planet is so far ahead of anything ever experienced by man that he would have to grope his way very slowly at first, in order to learn the lessons which such a high state of refined existence could teach him. This is one reason why it is so necessary for a male and female inhabitant of these Planets to act as his custodians, possibly for thousands of years, while he is evolving through the essential sets of experiences which form the foundations of such advanced cultures.

"The next step, which is the second part of this Freedom, results in an introduction into the Planet Venus or the Planet Uranus, where different experiences are gained."

It would appear that Venus and Uranus are on a higher plane of existence, are more advanced Spiritually and culturally than Pluto, Mars, Jupiter and Neptune. In fact during your study of the recommended literature, you will see that the Martians refer to the Venusians with the greatest possible respect and reverence. This attitude seems to convey the impression that Venus, and according to the text, Uranus, are inhabited by more highly Evolved Beings than most other Planets. But even should this be the case, it happens many times that the people from other Planets do visit Venus and Uranus in order to learn, even though they may not actually be a part of that particular cycle. Indeed, the next statement from the text points out that there is an interchange of population between all of these Planets.

"Interplanetary man is no longer bound to the clay of Terra or the clay of any other Planet. He is free to serve throughout the Galaxy—even outside of the Galaxy."

If a man or woman from another Planet comes on to Earth in their normal physical body, they are not bound to stay on Earth. They can move on or off the globe at will. The text tells us that the same is true of any Planet which they may inhabit. Not only can Interplanetary man move freely from Planet to Planet performing the particular Service which he has agreed to undertake, but he can go even outside of the Galaxy. It is known that the Martians, as well as the Venusians, have traveled the hundreds of light-years necessary in order to penetrate the confines of the Galaxy in which we live, and they have even made extra-Galactic probes to other Universes beyond.

"He does not pay lip service to anything existent, or non-existent, but begins to be a knower; begins to realize the 'why' of existence. Already he knows the 'how'—and so with his travel comes broadness."

The scientist studies "how" and according to Higher Wisdom, if he makes these studies in a purely materialistic way, he will only learn the "how." The philosopher studies the "why" and again, according to the great Minds, if he makes his studies through contemplation and Meditation, he begins to be a knower. In other words, he does not have to take for granted what others tell him, but knows the difference between right and wrong because he has tapped the great forces within himself. To a limited extent, even terrestrial man, who has mastered the ancient mystic science of Meditation, becomes a knower, so that he does not need to believe or disbelieve anything which is told to him, without applying the problem to his Meditations. This ability to be a knower is much more accentuated in Interplanetary man because of his previous cycles of experience.

"No longer is he even limited to a base physical structure, for he discovers that by excitation of the internal molecular working he can form this base structure into finer matter which he can propel through full Space."

Here we have some intimation of the Powers attained by Interplanetary man. It is possible for some advanced Adepts upon this Earth to project from a physical structure in full consciousness, travel to a certain place and come back with a full and complete memory of all they saw. Now conscious projection is a very rare ability, developed only by a few on this Earth. But Interplanetary man is capable of a feat much more advanced than a projection from the body. He is able to make his physical structure, although much finer than that of Earth man, even finer still, so tenuous in fact that he can consciously propel it throughout Space. In other words, Interplanetary man realizes that his physical structure can be used as a little Spacecraft which he can modify at will. For instance, in order to propel a physical structure throughout Space, he would have to be able to live without food and gasses, as we know them. His structure would have to be so finely balanced that it would have to live directly on the magnetic streams of Universal Life Force which flow through the Ether. The structure would also have to be so fine that it would be no longer affected by intense cold, or even, possibly, intense heat. In other words, the physical structure would have to be at least as fine as the etheric structure of the terrestrial Master. When we consider that such a refinement of matter is brought about consciously by Interplanetary man, possibly without outside help, we have some little idea of the enhanced powers of concentration and also the great technical ability of those people existing on a much higher level of consciousness. Such ability far surpasses anything ever accomplished by terrestrial man on Earth (Note 3).

"He begins to work towards the perfect singular Vortex and the perfect Vacuum."

Interplanetary man begins to transfer all of his energies up to the highest Vortex or Crown Chakra and strictly control them within this centre, so that he may eventually attain the state of perfect Vacuum. A perfect Vacuum is, of course, true simplicity which is a state of "nothingness," above any manifested state. All manifestation is a deviation from simplicity or, to put it another way, the result of opposing forces which have been introduced into the original state of pure potential. The nearer one evolves towards perfect simplicity, the unmanifested state of pure potential, the nearer one gets towards the one perfect simple or The Absolute (Note 4).

"He is capable of experience in more than one system of dimension at the same instant."

On Thursday, December 6th, 1957, the author had the privilege of making a contact with an important Cosmic Master. During this meeting, the Master gave a brilliant definition of the seven dimensions in which all things exist. The following is an exact quotation of this unique revelation.

"Now, manifestation could not exist without a Power which is capable of creating the tension necessary to hold the particles of matter in a certain state which constitutes the nucleus of sub-atomic and atomic structure. This Power utilizes energy and is capable of imposing certain limits upon the energy of motion. The Power which imposes direction upon motion is—mind! Now, mind by itself is an all-pervasive energy which, for the sake of simplicity, you could term as a pattern of potential. A pattern which, to all intents, is static until pressures are applied from outside, which dictate direction to it. Therefore, manifestation exists within this framework: Will, mind, motion, time, length, breadth and height.

"The Divine Will imposes those conditions upon mind which bring its potential into manifestation as directed motion in a time-frame of length, breadth and height. "Of course, this is but a simplified version of a profound concept, as you no doubt see. Divine Will cannot Itself be measured, for It is above and beyond its own manifestation but we do have some idea of the basic function of this Power. There are even 'sub' states, such as feeling, which I have purposely avoided in order to simplify your explanation of the subject." (Extract taken from *Cosmic Voice* Issue No. 14, published in February, 1958, by The Aetherius Press, London, England.)

This outstanding definition should give the thinking student some appreciation of the seven dimensional framework in which he exists. But no matter how profound his Meditative abilities, he cannot, at this stage of his Evolution, conceive of other systems of dimension which are co-existent with this (Note 5).

But Interplanetary man is capable of such a realization and also capable of experience within other dimensions the like of which terrestrial man is unable to conceive.

"As he goes deeper into this Freedom, he realizes his great Power as a ray capable of the manifestation of thought visualizations. He becomes a tiny thought Creator. He learns to control his visualizations so that they conform exactly to predetermined patterns."

In your study of "Glory of Ascension" at the end of Chapter 6, you will see that the Master from Venus, who actually performed the Initiation, wore a girdle studded with crystals. You will also note the Martian's comments upon the function of this crystal belt.

The text states that Interplanetary man, after he has gained certain necessary experiences, learns how to become a thought Creator. The crystal belt which he wears has certain definite attributes, one of the most important of which is that it acts as a magnet which draws together the Pranas or Universal Life Forces out of which all things are formed. The Interplanetary Adept is capable of very concentrated thought and visualization. The Pranas drawn together into this crystal battery are then formed into the picture which he visualizes, giving it form and shape and actual physical manifestation. This is far above the capabilities of an Earth Master who is only able to form his visualizations in mind substance. The Interplanetary Master is capable of bringing these visualizations into physical, living and breathing manifestation and keeping them in being as long as is necessary in order to perform the particular function for which they were specifically designed. After this, like the true White Magician that he is, he would take them out of manifestation again by another type of manipulation, drawing the visualization back into himself through the solar plexus centre. This is one of the secrets of White Magic and it is an important one inasmuch as every picturization or thought form sent out, whether made of mind substance or formed into a physical manifestation, must be taken back again by the magician if he wishes to retain his Powers. This is well worth remembering.

It is also worth remembering that if a negative visualization is sent forth, this thought form is liable to work against those who project it and should immediately be taken out of manifestation by causing it to be withdrawn through the solar plexus centre so that it does not continue along its destructive way. Even a Spiritual visualization should, after its function has been performed, be absorbed back in this way if the magician is to keep his Power. All living beings may be classed as magicians for all thought and action is really an act of, either black, grey or White Magic (Note 6).

Interplanetary man knows the Laws of Creative White Magic and strictly abides by them.

"He would rather give up even his present Freedom and be cast into the lowest terrestrial astral realms, than disobey his Masters, by even a glance—by even a glance!"

The text here asserts, in a very pointed way, the absolute necessity for obedience to the highest Forces, if any degree of Freedom is to be

gained. One of the secrets of success in all active Metaphysical practice, is a complete obedience to the Teachings of one's Master as well
as strict adherence to the all-pervasive Law. When terrestrial man has
learned this one fact, his Evolution will follow a surer, less erratic
course than it does at present.

When the lifestream has gone through the experience necessary to
become Interplanetary man, it will realize the necessity of self-discipline and strict obedience. No degree of Freedom, which is
Enlightenment, can be gained without the imposition of self-discipline by the student. He must choose a Master whose teachings seem
right to him and LIVE by those teachings. He must be prepared to
give up his own petty freewill upon the altar of strict obedience to
the instruction of a person obviously wiser than himself, if he is, eventually, to reflect that same Light of Wisdom himself. Interplanetary
man realizes that he is in his present exalted position as much by the
grace of the Wise Ones, as by his own efforts. Therefore, he would
rather sacrifice his salvation than disobey his Masters by even a
glance, as the text says, or if you wish by even a thought. This is one
of the secrets of success. Earthman will never gain success in Spiritual
matters until he adopts the same outlook. No one can ever really
reach the lofty heights of true Evolvement until he is able to treat as
Sacred the greater Wisdom which is propounded by his Master. Of
this there is no doubt. When Truth means this much to a man, he will
find it—but not until then.

*"He does not worship his Masters because of their Power, but
because They are a reflection of the Divine Principle."*

Interplanetary man sees, in his Masters from Saturn, a truer, less discoloured reflection of God or The Absolute, than he sees within
himself. That is why he worships these Great Ones, because They
have traveled much further along the road than he has, back to Their
Divine Source. In other words, he worships God in all Its Greatness,
through one of the manifestations of God. After all, that is the end of
the capability of intelligence if we really examine it in a logical
manner. Man upon Earth thinks that he can worship an abstraction.
He cannot do so. When he becomes more advanced he finds that he
can only worship God through Its manifestations. This secret of
Evolution has been learned by Interplanetary man.

All students will profit greatly by giving these statements their deepest consideration. Success or failure will depend upon this!

"Know this: the wheel turns twice and the red globe dispels the darkness, so that the yellow globe may rise. In the rising comes— realization. When the blue globe intersects the yellow globe at the right angle—consciousness is born. When the green globe causes fusion between the two, realization of consciousness takes place and all the colours are manifest. When the violet globe rises into the Golden Sphere, the crescent of Wisdom is born and—shineth."

This is a symbolic statement of deep profundity given to more advanced students so that they may apply it to their Meditations. It is known that only when applied to Meditation, can this profound statement reveal much. So therefore, it is not fitting that any full explanation should be attempted at this point. However, a framework of Truth may tend to guide the student into the correct Meditative conclusion which he, eventually, must arrive at himself.

In the beginning there was darkness, there was profound silence and yet, in this dark silence there was the whole of manifestation in a state of dormant potential. For some reason known only to Divine Intelligence, The Absolute saw fit to realize this potential and bring it into active manifestation. This was done by the introduction of certain forces which caused, as their reaction, the manifestation of the original potential which was The Absolute in Its pure state. The Divine Will of The Absolute imposed certain conditions upon original potential or latent mind which brought this potential into manifestation as directed motion in a time-frame of length, breadth and height. Here we have the seven dimensions in which we all exist. The symbology of the text states that The Absolute involved Itself so that the almost infinite cycle of involution away from and Evolution back to its Divine Source could take place. This seems the only logical explanation for the existence of Evolution. The Absolute in Its unmanifested state is plu-perfection, therefore cannot be Evolved because no higher state than this is possible. Therefore, in order to make Evolution possible, involution must first have been directed by The Absolute. Some mystic texts refer to this as the "out-breathing and in-breathing" of the Initial Creator. The "out-breathing" being the apparent individualization of The Absolute when It involved or created all forms of life down to the very lowest. The "in-breathing" being the recalling or Evolution of all things back into Itself again.

This seems to be the only logical explanation which gives any real meaning to manifestation.

It is interesting to note the particular colours used in the symbology. The "red globe" symbolizes the forces which caused, as a reaction, a basic form of manifestation—possibly atomic. As yellow is the symbolic colour denoting intelligence—when these forces were activated, further realization of the original potential took place. Blue is the symbolic colour of higher intelligence. The "blue globe" intersected the "yellow globe" at the right angle, then consciousness was born. Then the "green globe" caused fusion between the two and then realization of consciousness took place. Green is the colour of balance as it is in the middle of the spectrum. Therefore, such forces would cause fusion or a balance between intelligence and higher intelligence, causing realization of self-consciousness as expressed in the life form called man and those life forms above man. The "violet globe" is symbolic of Super-Consciousness. When this rises into the: "Golden Sphere, the crescent of Wisdom is born and—shineth!" This is a symbolic way of stating that, as it does in Meditation, there comes a stage when the Soul is bathed in the Light of the Spirit, the Spirit being symbolically represented in the text as the—"Golden Sphere." This apparently individualized part of The Absolute, being pure potential, has within It all knowledge and all manifestation. When this state comes about then the Meditator becomes one with that upon which he Meditates and Wisdom is born.

This outline is not given as a full interpretation of the profound symbology but rather, as previously stated, to form a framework serving as a guide for future Meditation.

> *"This is the secret of—Creation.*
> *"It is the secret of—Preservation.*
> *"It is the secret of Transmutation.*
> *"It is the Sacred Word—A-U-M."*

Of all the great Truths revealed in The Nine Freedoms, this is one of the most staggering to the advanced occultist, for it puts a new light upon the ancient Wisdom. THERE ARE MANY ADVANCED MINDS WHO WOULD NOT HAVE BELIEVED SUCH A FEAT POSSIBLE, for the more advanced the student of The Nine Freedoms, the more he will be absolutely staggered by this part of the text. Here is the deepest Wisdom yet given to Earth, illustrated in a simple, yet profound way for all of you to appreciate.

In order to understand this better the student is referred to Plate 7. In the illustration, you will see the great Creative WORD, symbolized by a sixty degree triangle representing Wisdom and also the interpretation of this WORD, given by inspiration, thousands of centuries ago by the Ancient Seers. First let us examine the WORD itself. The A-U-M does not belong to any language because it is the basis of all language. No man, or any other living thing upon this Earth, can make any sound outside this one sound. All language that we now use, or ever have, or ever will use upon this Planet, is made up of the numerous parts of this one single sound. No notes ever sung, nor Mantras ever chanted, are outside of this one sonic framework. If we examine this in a more detailed fashion, we will be able to see why this is so.

In order to chant this WORD you must use the full sound capabilities of the larynx and tongue. The -A- starts right the way back in the throat, with the tongue put down in the mouth. The -U- comes toward the centre of the larynx with the tongue stretched a little further forward and curled so that this sound is made in the middle of the mouth and on the middle of the tongue. The -M- sound is made in the front of the mouth with the tongue pushed right forward. Therefore, in order to make this sound, it is necessary to use the full capabilities of the larynx, aided by the tongue, with the whole roof of the mouth acting as a sounding board. As the utterance of this one, all-inclusive sound demands the full use of man's natural sound-making system, THEN ALL THE PARTS OF SPOKEN LANGUAGES ARE BUT FRACTIONAL PARTS OF THIS ONE WORD. The whole must be greater than the part. A few moments reflection will teach the student that this is the only full sound he, or any other man, is able to make with his mouth, and all other sounds are but parts of this whole.

This is the WORD which was with GOD in the beginning.

There is a time in Meditation when the student will hear the tremendous Creative forces which are emanated by the Sun each thirty-two minutes, when each of the five major Pranas changes its form and state throughout the day and night. This is the sound of continual Creation which is always taking place. The Ancient Seers, who first heard this, recognized it as the sound of Creation and they gave the major stages of involution and Evolution of life, as shown in the second illustration in Plate 7.

At the apex of the sixty degree triangle, depicting Wisdom in manifestation, we have Creation. This is The Absolute. The Absolute saw fit to involve Itself in what we call matter and at the bottom of the triangle we can see the introduction of the negative pole of Preservation. Through the multitudinous states of Preservation, the Soul, entombed in matter, moves until finally it passes through the Initiation of Transmigration when, according to the Ancients, it left matter and became pure Spirit to travel again back through Evolution, gradually simplifying itself until it became Creation again, or joined with the One Creative Force or the Initial Cause (Special Note).

Now, if we look at Plate 8, we see a much fuller and a much truer explanation of what is known to happen. We have the Sacred WORD—A-U-M represented by the triangle of Wisdom, with the sixty degree angles of Creation. The second illustration in Plate 8, shows us again the triangle, symbolic of the Creative Power at the apex of the triangle, wrapping itself in matter, being preserved by the negative Creative force, or the force of Preservation travelling through the multitudinous expressions, until—and this is the staggering facet introduced by the Master Who gave this text—it passes through, not as the Ancients stated the Initiation of Transmigration, but the INITIATION OF TRANSMUTATION. In other words, life, coming from the Initial Creative Source, passes through numerous experiences and returns to the Initial Creative Source again, but with the energy gained from the complete Transmutation of all matter up to the highest conceivable level. Only after it has gained the knowledge to cause a complete Transmutation of matter upon the Highest possible planes can it become attached again to the Creative Source.

The initial interpretation showed the Soul being taken from matter and travelling back to the Source after using matter as a vehicle of experience. No attempt was made by the Ancients to say what happened to the enormous energy which constituted the matter itself. If it remained on the level which it had been involved down to, then it would be outside of the Law of Evolution and this aspect of The Absolute would not be all inclusive, therefore incomplete. The interpretation by Mars Sector 6 states that the Soul does not transmigrate, or break away from matter, but causes a complete Transmutation or Spiritualization of matter which it has used as a vehicle of expression, and takes this Spiritualized mass back to the Creative Force again with it, at the end of the journey through total expression, which is Evolution. There is no doubt that this is a complete explanation of Life's journey from perfection, through involution, through Evolution, back to perfection again. How else could Life express itself fully unless it was capable of the Spiritualization of all things, including the material vehicle it has used, in order to gain this expression and experience? Logic will tell you that this must be the answer, that this statement will stand the one sure acid test of Truth upon this world— Meditation upon it.

If nothing else had been given in the mystic text of *The Nine Freedoms* save these four sentences, then it would still rank as one of the greatest and most important texts ever delivered to Earth.

The author would like to point out it is his belief that this information was given in this descriptive way rather because the world is now ready for it, than because the Ancients had made any mistake. It is not believed that the meaning of the Creative WORD was not understood by the Seers, but that the world was ready only for the explanation which They gave at that time. Now, as the world stands upon the verge of the final Initiation into the Age of Enlightenment, the Master has now given a fuller, more descriptive Truth to those people upon Earth, who are ready for it (Note 7).

The next sentences in the text give some indication of the tremendous importance of this Wisdom:

"Your internal vibrations have been altered by these utterances. Do not ever slip from the path for if you do, your fall will be doubly hard."

It should be pointed out that the whole philosophical and religious concept of man is summed up in the previous few sentences, hence their immeasurable importance to everyone on Earth now and those who will reincarnate in the future. So vital is this information that, once man has been exposed to it, he has a greater responsibility towards his essential part in the Cosmic Scheme than he had previously. So great is this responsibility that if, after exposure to this most vital Truth of all, the student then slips badly from the path, his fall will be doubly hard. It is known that the higher up the ladder of Evolution one climbs, the more difficult are the tests which one has to endure and also the more subtle are the temptations which are dangled before such a climber.

After the most careful consideration, and in deference to the generosity displayed by the remarkable Mars Sector 6, Who, in compassion, gave this profound Wisdom, it should be made clear to all students that those who have read this far have BEEN GRANTED AN INITIATION INTO THE HIGHEST ASPECT OF METAPHYSICAL TRUTH YET GIVEN TO MANKIND IN THE PRESENT OR ANY PREVIOUS LIFE ON EARTH!

You have gained not only greater Enlightenment through this Initiation, but more important still, a framework of Wisdom upon which you can base your further contemplations and Meditations. Because you have been mentally and Spiritually armed in this way, you have advanced greatly and your temptations to leave the path of Truth will be more subtle than before, but your strength and determination to progress should be greater than ever. When the Master gives the warning in the text, He means exactly what He states.

This is the most important Truth yet revealed to you. It has been made understandable for you. Use it as a guide so that you may be led towards a deeper awareness within yourself, but guard yourself well. No matter how rough the road through progress becomes, stick courageously to it and if you do so, you will Bless Almighty God for guiding you to the Wisdom you have just been Initiated into. This is known to the Masters.

Sooner or later this will be known by you also.

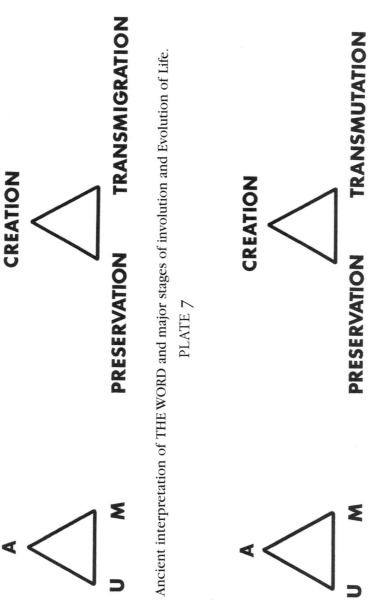

CREATION

TRANSMIGRATION

PRESERVATION

A

M

U

Ancient interpretation of THE WORD and major stages of involution and Evolution of Life.

PLATE 7

CREATION

TRANSMUTATION

PRESERVATION

A

M

U

Latest and much fuller interpretation of THE WORD and the involution and Evolution of Life.

PLATE 8

AUTHOR'S RECOMMENDATIONS

NOTE 1. See the Metaphysical lesson, *The Seven Dimensions Of Creation*, for a better understanding of this profound Truth.

NOTE 2. Read *Life On The Planets*, for further information regarding the accomplishments of Interplanetary Intelligences.

NOTE 3. Read *You Are Responsible!* (pages 127-144) for further information regarding Mars and Venus.
A close study of the Metaphysical lesson, *The Four Aspects Of Creation*, will unravel one of the most intriguing mysteries of the Beings from other Planets.

NOTE 4. A careful study of "Cosmic Logic," in *You Are Responsible!* is highly recommended. There you have a brilliant dissertation on simplicity, as delivered by a great Master from the Planet Venus.

NOTE 5. See the Metaphysical lesson, *The Seven Dimensions Of Creation*, for a complete explanation of the revelation of the seven dimensions in which all things exist.

NOTE 6. Study of the Metaphysical lesson, *The Three Forms Of Magic*, will help the student to differentiate between each form of magic so that he only performs that which is of the highest possible Spiritual order.

NOTE 7. Read "The Initiation Of Earth," in *You Are Responsible!* (pages 145-159) for more complete details issued by Higher Authority regarding the coming Millennium.

All above books and Metaphysical lessons are available from the publishers of *The Nine Freedoms* at www.aetherius.org.

SPECIAL NOTE. This sums up in a few words the framework upon which the *Bhagavad Gita* was written. A study of this book is well worthwhile, especially if the student keeps in mind the latest interpretation of Evolution given in *The Nine Freedoms*.

CHAPTER 8

THE EIGHTH FREEDOM WILL BE SATURNIAN EXISTENCE

SAINT GOO-LING

"By Power vested in Me, I sacrifice this Prasad to Brahma. I sacrifice all to Brahma. It is Blessed.

"Afterwards dispense to all.

"Now, at beginning of Nine Freedoms, your Leader made appeal on behalf of all who came that you should receive little Cross Blessed by Master Jesus. This request will be granted at end of Ninth Freedom. Master Jesus will, acting through your Leader, cause Crosses to be Blessed. If for any reason you cannot attend at that time, Cross then must be kept for you. Must not be sent, but must be given to you.

"You are fortunate that you have Leader able to make demand in such a way that difficult to say, no.

"Knock upon door of inner Flame, sooner or later will be opened and God Presence will manifest through all of you.

"You have all tried best to act as channels for Power which has been sent out during this Operation. Much Power has been sent out, both by you and by people in other countries. Try again this time and next time, so that Operation might be successfully completed.

"I go."

MARS SECTOR 6

"This is Mars Sector 6 reporting from Satellite No. 3, now in Magnetization Orbit—Terra, during Magnetization Period No. 1, present phase.

"The Eighth Freedom will be—SATURNIAN EXISTENCE.

"After the Lifestream has gained experience by living and serving

159

on other Planets in the Solar System, It is then ready to be introduced into an even greater, fuller, more complete, more aware cycle of existence. It is presented to the Lesser Solar Lords for Initiation. After this Initiation, It is then introduced into the Saturnian Life cycle. At this time, It is neither male nor female, but both, in the highest possible sense.

"The Saturnian cycle starts with an introduction through the Logos of the Planet Itself into Saturnian Service. From here, the Lifestream gradually advances until It is ready to be introduced into the Primary Life Cycle of that Planet. It enters this Primary Life Cycle as a Cosmic Master and gradually becomes amalgamated with another Lifestream, vibrating in nearly the same manner, until It becomes six-fold.

"Then, after serious Initiation, It is confined to—Timelessness. Realization is born.

"The next major Initiation causes a division between this Lifestream and all others. It travels to some place outside of the Solar System and spends the equivalent of 125,000 of your terrestrial years in Meditation. After this, It returns to Saturn—full proven.

"From there, It goes into the Primary Hall of Initiation upon the Sun to receive the Secret Doctrines. It returneth to Its Planet and as a Light of the Supreme Interplanetary Council, It shineth.

"Such a One has no individuality as such—for It is all individual; has no sex as such—for It is twice female, twice male and twice neither.

"Such a One has a still body, which moves not.

"Such a One is capable of a division of consciousness which allows It to inhabit up to 1,860 positions in the space-time continuum at one and the same instant! In fact, some of the Perfects are able to double this feat.

"Such a One is not limited—because of limitation.

"Such a One has great Freedom—because It has rejected all freedom.

"Such a One has access to all mind—because It has consciously and super-consciously, on the Intuitive levels, rejected all mind.

"Such a One is an active blood vessel in the arm of The Absolute.

"Such a One is a Flame of everlasting Inspiration.

"Such a One is all silent—and yet all sound, is stillness—and yet all movement, is a single entity, made up of the amalgamation of two—and yet is all entities.

"Such a One as this is beyond description.

"It is the Flame.

"It is the guiding Light, which shows us all, the way through our darkness.

"It is an enactment of supreme sacrifice—everlasting Service.

"It is a great and mighty existent Intelligence on its way to a complete amalgamation with—Divinity Itself.

"Such a One is High, even in the opinions of the Logoi.

"This is Freedom. This Freedom is offered unto all lifestreams. It depends upon the effort they expend as to whether or not they will approach this goal in billions of trillions of lives, or whether they will accomplish these things in less time.

"Such a One as this is revered by us all, for through such a Being as this, shines a Spark of The Absolute—a Spark of The Absolute which we can see for ourselves; for we cannot see The Absolute Itself, only Its Manifestation.

"Such a One as this is revered beyond all description; beyond all word; beyond all thought. If such a One as this says, "Nay," it is that. For It speaketh in the wise tongue of silence—yet It speaketh.

"These are the Masters of the Planetary System, Who are actively engaged in helping all lifestreams to evolve out of their darkness, their ignorance, their suffering.

"The Eighth Freedom is brought about by sustained effort.

"By obedience.

"By dedication beyond all description.

"By Service.

"By the dispensation of true Love.

"By controlled thought, controlled action, controlled inaction.

"By raising the Kundalini fully upwards.

"By Cosmic Consciousness.

"By conscious Ascension.

"By Interplanetary experience.

"And by amalgamation into the Whole.

"The wheel turned twice and consciousness was born.

"The wheel turned four times and consciousness evolved up to Interplanetary levels.

"The wheel turned 1,980 times and consciousness was evolved up to secondary Saturnian level.

"The wheel turned 9,458 times and consciousness was evolved up to Primary Saturnian level.

"Take this into the silence with you. You will be better when you come out of it.

"All Transmissions now discontinued."

Delivered on Sunday, March 12th, 1961.

SATURNIAN EXISTENCE

Once again Prasad was Blessed by Saint Goo-Ling before The Eighth Freedom and was later dispensed to all the invited audience. After Blessing the Prasad, Saint Goo-Ling made a reference to the coming ceremony of charging the small wooden Crosses. This ceremony will be described more fully in the next chapter.

"The Eighth Freedom will be—SATURNIAN EXISTENCE.
"After the Lifestream has gained experience by living and serving on other Planets in the Solar System, It is then ready to be introduced into an even greater, fuller, more complete, more aware cycle of existence."

You read in Chapters 6 and 7 how a lifestream, after passing through the necessary experiences on this Earth, is given the Initiation of Ascension and how from there the first Planetary step is taken as an introduction into the life cycle of either Mars, Neptune, Jupiter or Pluto. The student should be reminded that the lifestream will have to have experience on all of these Planets, and will have to move between one Planet and another, and indeed, does so quite freely. Then the Intelligence progresses towards an introduction into the life cycle of Venus and Uranus, where different, essential lessons are learned. When sufficient Cosmic experience has been gained by the Lifestream, It is then deemed ready for the next important and decisive step through Evolution.

"It is presented to the Lesser Solar Lords for Initiation. After this Initiation, It is then introduced into the Saturnian life cycle. At this time, It is neither male nor female, but both, in the highest possible sense."

The Lesser Solar Lords are the Initiating Lords Who inhabit the Sun. These are the great Beings Who deem whether or not the Lifestream is ready for the introduction into the Saturnian life cycle. Should the Lords declare that the Intelligence is ready for this introduction, They make preparations for and perform the actual Cosmic Initiation of the tested Lifestream. The text states that at this time the Lifestream is neither male nor female, but both in the highest possible sense. This means that the Interplanetary Intelligence is now a perfectly balanced Being, being male Creative and female Preservative, also having a complete balance between these two major polarities. The Intelligence has complete control over Creative and Preservative abilities and is not subject to imbalance such as that found in both male and female upon Earth.

"The Saturnian cycle starts with an introduction through the Logos of the Planet—Itself into Saturnian Service."
The Lifestream is introduced into the Saturnian life cycle rather in the same way that It was previously introduced into other Planetary life cycles. It is born as an adult through the Logos, or Life Force of the Planet Saturn, which, like all other Planets, is actually a living Entity.

"From here, the Lifestream gradually advances until It is ready to be introduced into the Primary Life Cycle of that Planet."
The first introduction into Saturnian existence may be termed an introduction into the secondary life cycle of this Planet. The text states that much experience is necessary before the Intelligence, even with Its vast Planetary experience, can be introduced into the Primary, or more active, Life Cycle of Saturn. Later in the text you will see that there is a tremendous Evolutionary difference between these two particular life cycles, even though they occur on the same Planet, in, what we may assume to be, similar environmental conditions.

"It enters this Primary Life Cycle as a Cosmic Master and gradually becomes amalgamated with another Lifestream, vibrating in nearly the same manner, until It becomes sixfold."
This is a very interesting point and one of the most profound occult Truths ever given to this Earth at any time. The Intelligence, after gaining sufficient experience in the secondary life cycle of the Planet Saturn, then enters the Primary Life Cycle as a fully-fledged Cosmic Master. Now, the text stated earlier that the Evolved Lifestream is neither male nor female, but both, in other words, It is a three-fold Being. It is male, positive Creative; female, negative Preservative and that perfect balance between these two mental polarities. Here we have a reference that It amalgamates completely with another Lifestream, vibrating in nearly the same manner. As both Lifestreams are three-fold Intelligences, when They amalgamate together They naturally become a six-fold Intelligence. We are

informed that They both vibrate in nearly, not exactly, but nearly the same manner as one another. They obviously vibrate as nearly on the same frequency as it is possible for any two Lifestreams to vibrate. So the amalgamation then causes a double male, Creative positive force and a double female, negative Preservative force and a double balance between these two forces. In other words, a six-fold Being.

"The next major Initiation causes a division between this Lifestream and all others. It travels to some place outside of the Solar System and spends the equivalent of 125,000 of your terrestrial years in Meditation. After this, It returns to Saturn—fully proven."

This six-fold Being, after a certain set of experiences, after possibly the equivalent of hundreds of thousands of terrestrial years in Service, not only upon Saturn, but also upon other Planets as well, works towards another very serious type of Initiation. It then leaves the Solar System entirely and travels to some environment which has not been mentioned in the text, because of its secret significance, where the Being spends the equivalent of 125,000 years in Meditation.

It is very difficult for any of us to fully appreciate such a feat. How an Intelligence could be so advanced as to be capable of holding Meditation for this length of time, not one of us here has even the remotest idea. It is believed that this statement was put in the text to illustrate the wide difference between a Lifestream capable of existing in the Saturnian Evolutionary cycle and one capable of existing in the Evolutionary cycle of Earth. It is believed that here is a pattern, a definite pointer to us all, a small glimpse of the eventual destination of all lifestreams in the Solar System, even those from the infant class, which is this Earth. It should also be remembered by the student, that information such as that given in this text has never been divulged before. These amazing Truths were given at this time, in order to bring about as much rise in man's consciousness as possible, just prior to the Initiation of Earth, which must reach a climax before long (Note 1).

"From here, It goes into the Primary Hall of Initiation upon the Sun to receive the Secret Doctrines. It returneth to Its Planet and as a Light of the Supreme Interplanetary Council, It shineth."

After being sent into virtual timelessness for the equivalent of 125,000 years of deep Meditation, the Lifestream then travels to the Primary Hall of Initiation upon the physical Sun of our Solar System. After being Initiated into the Secret Doctrines, and no one on Earth has even the slightest conception what these are, It is then ready to be elected to the Supreme Interplanetary Council.

It must be remembered, that this Earth is the only Planet in the Solar System which is not represented in the Interplanetary Tribunal which exists upon Saturn.

This is a governing body, but not governing in the same way that we know political bodies upon Earth to be governing. It is really an Advisory Body consisting of highly Evolved Beings of proven experience and elevated Cosmic Status, Who are ready to initiate and advise. Beings, Who manipulate the higher forces which exist, unbeknown to mere man, in this Solar System. Beings, Who obviously work as Agents for the Lords of Karma so that the great Law can function in its pluperfect manner.

"Such a One is capable of a division of consciousness which allows It to inhabit up to 1,860 positions in the space-time continuum at one and the same instant! In fact, some of the Perfects are able to double this feat."

We cannot yet even begin to appreciate such a feat. However, some limited type of understanding can be brought about if we imagine one of the Beings of Saturn, probably 30 to 40 feet in height, remaining absolutely immobile for thousands of years, in a body which is shaped like a huge incandescent ovoid, wrapped in deep Cosmic Meditation and yet, at the same time, being capable of making for Itself 1,860 other bodies, operating them on other worlds, and being in full knowledge and control of each of these bodies at one and the same time. This will give some idea of the stupendous Power and vast intellectual capabilities of the great Masters of Saturn.

Reference in the text to the space-time continuum means that these would still be physical bodies, even though they may be made up of a physical structure different from our particular bodies upon Earth. The text also states that the Perfects are capable of twice this feat (Note 2).

By His reference here to the Perfects, Mars Sector 6 denotes the Twelve guiding Lights in the Interplanetary Council upon Saturn.

They can, according to the text, divide Their Consciousness into 3,720 different parts and send these different bodies on to 3,720 different inhabited or uninhabited worlds throughout the Galaxy and be fully conscious and in control of each and every part at one and the same instant.

Here is Truth, much more fantastic than any fiction yet written.

"Such a One is not limited because of limitation."

Such a One has Freedom beyond man's wildest imagination, because of carefully disciplined limitation It has set upon Itself, throughout countless lives of experience.

There is a world of difference between Freedom and freewill. It is by the use of his freewill that man on Earth commits the crimes he does, puts upon himself the limitations that he has put upon himself; holds himself back in the way that he does. Sooner or later all men must realize this. Those who have already done so have begun to discipline themselves. They have taken the first main step in applied Metaphysics, which is to control the vital life fluid—the sex fluid (Note 3). By this discipline they have, of course, curbed their freewill, they have curbed their petty freedom. But the result, of even this one particular discipline, is a greater Freedom than they have ever experienced before; a keener mental alertness, a surer balance. The text states, that the only way to bring about true Freedom is by the imposition of strict self-discipline, which is necessary to guarantee further progress.

Let us take another illustration; Meditation for instance. The Meditator cannot move, he is paralyzed. He is hardly breathing; his heart is just beating, he is almost dead; he has disciplined himself until he can sit completely immobile. This action has curbed his petty freewill—but what of his Freedom? He can soar to the highest planes! He can become conscious and live through experiences which he has never dreamed possible before he imposed these disciplines. He has a greater Freedom than ever he had before, and ever he will have until the next time he enters the Meditative state. In the passage and that which follows, the Master is pointing out to us, that the way to true Freedom is through the rejection of our own petty freedoms, which we hold on to so belligerently on this Earth.

"Such a One has great Freedom—because It has rejected all freedom."

Here we have a definite and logical illustration which proves the point. It is a statement of irrevocable Truth and, like all statements of Truth, it appears to be paradoxical.

"Such a One has access to all mind—because It has consciously and Super-Consciously, on the Intuitive levels, rejected all mind."
Another illustration of the paradox of Truth. It is a certain fact, that if you reject any aspect of Nature, then it will, in some strange way, pour its very fruits at your feet. If you consciously control your mind, you bring about the ability to concentrate. If you consciously control even the ability to concentrate, you bring about the ability to contemplate. If you consciously control your contemplative ability and stop your conscious brain from any apparent action at all, then you will open your super-conscious brain up to even greater Power, wider Freedom such as that experienced in Meditation. If you could then take the next step, which is the rejection of even the results of deep Meditation, you would be opened up to a state more glorious and elevated than even that experienced in deep Meditation. However, even to an Adept on Earth, this last step is only pure theory, for he is incapable of taking it. The text tells us that the Beings on Saturn are capable of occult feats which defy any explanation which could be given of them at this stage.

"Such a One is all silent—and yet all sound."
We have been informed that such a Being has a still Body and yet can split Its Consciousness into hundreds of different parts. The still Body is all silent. It does not move. But the hundreds of parts into which It is capable of dividing Its Consciousness, are all sound. In other words, can make hundreds of different sounds, hear hundreds of different sounds, become acutely aware of the reaction caused by these hundreds of sounds at one and the same instant.

"Is stillness—and yet all movement."
The main point of consciousness of the Being is the radiantly incandescent ovoid body which stays completely still yet, without moving this point of consciousness, It can split Itself up into all movement.

"Is a single Entity made up of the amalgamation of Two—yet is all entities."
Has a single point of consciousness and yet, if the Being is One of

the Twelve Perfects of Saturn, It can split this consciousness up into almost four thousand different, fully conscious entities; in other words, is all entities.

"It is the Flame."
It points always back to Its Divine Source, of which It becomes acutely aware. Like all other flames, It will not point downwards, but always upwards, always striving to rise ever—upwards.

"It is the guiding Light which shows us all, the way through our darkness."
The Beings on Saturn have formed Themselves into an Advisory Council to which, those who have been accepted into the Interplanetary Council of inhabited worlds, send their most highly Evolved Masters, so that They may receive advice, guidance and help from the Saturnians, who give this freely. Indeed, these Beings do show even Interplanetary people the way out of their problems.

"It is an enactment of supreme sacrifice—everlasting Service."
According to the "Upanishads," the greatest gift that one man can give to another is Wisdom. The greatest gift that a Saturnian Being can give to an Interplanetary man is the fruit of Its Wisdom, which has been gained through vast experience of solving unimaginably complex psycho-Spiritual problems. Such help is indeed, as the text states, "… an enactment of supreme sacrifice."

"This is Freedom. This Freedom is offered to all lifestreams. It depends upon the effort they expend as to whether or not they will approach this goal in billions of trillions of lives, or whether they will accomplish these things in less time."
Again we have a Cosmic promise, so startlingly great as to be beyond our meager powers of appreciation. Again we are reminded that Salvation—or Freedom, which is another word for it—is within our grasp, entirely dependent upon the effort we expend in order to bring it about. The number of lives taken to attain such Freedom is strictly within our control.

"Such a One as this is revered by us all, for through such a Being as this, shines a Spark of The Absolute—a Spark of The Absolute which we can see for ourselves; for we cannot see The Absolute

Itself—only Its manifestation."

No man or even Master can look into the face of God. All he can do is to worship God through One of Its multitudinous manifestations. The wise student is he who reveres his Master, not because of his superior mystical Powers, but because he sees there a truer reflection of the Holy Spark of God than he sees in himself.

This is the outlook of the wise student, the rare student, the one seldom found. Metaphysical students who, through the very careful use of their discrimination have found a really good teacher, adhere strictly to the lessons of that teacher, pay him the obvious reverence which his greater Wisdom and experience demand, are those students who progress quickly. No others can hope to advance as surely as these rare few until they too have learned this deep occult secret. The Ancients knew it. If you read some of the books from the east, written by the students of Masters of Yoga, you will see how they revere and Love their Masters in a manner which is beyond the capability of those generally found in the west. There is a great difference between the advancement of such unique students and that of the majority of those found in the west. The rare student's humility, WHICH ALLOWS HIM TO HOLD EVERY WORD SPOKEN BY HIS MASTER AS A SACRED UTTERANCE, accounts for this great difference.

Respect God-Truth and your Master if you wish to advance.

"These are the Masters of the Planetary System, Who are actively engaged in helping all lifestreams to Evolve out of their darkness, their ignorance, their suffering."

Without such Masters as these in the Planetary System, only God knows what it would be like. These Beings, realizing Their interrelationship with all other lifestreams, have forged ahead through unimaginably hard work and suffering, have Evolved to such a point that Their very existence within this Solar System helps to rise all other life forms within it. There is no Service greater than this which can possibly be imagined.

Every time a murder is committed on Earth, the mass of humanity is held back in some degree by that shameful crime committed by one of their number. As we are inter-related in the body of a whole, any disease in one cell affects that whole. On the other hand, any Enlightenment in one cell also affects that whole. Every lifestream on Earth is affected, in some degree, for the better by the existence of the great Beings upon Saturn. You would do well, always, to remember this.

If you must forget your name, do so, but NEVER FORGET THE DEBT YOU OWE TO THE MASTERS ON SATURN IF YOU ARE SEARCHING FOR AND HOPE TO FIND—ENLIGHTENMENT.

Remember also, that every good deed you do, every true Spiritual Prayer you send forth, every aspect of a true contemplation you give to man, every time that you enter the true Meditative state, you are helping, not only the few around you, but the mass of cells which help to make up this inter-related body of the whole.

"The wheel turned twice and consciousness was born. The wheel turned four times and consciousness Evolved up to Interplanetary levels. The wheel turned 1,980 times and consciousness was Evolved up to secondary Saturnian level. The wheel turned 9,458 times and consciousness was Evolved up to—Primary Saturnian level."

This is a very clever, yet very simple way, of illustrating the tremendous difference between these levels of consciousness.

Secondary Saturnian level of consciousness is 495 times more Evolved than Inter-Planetary level.

Primary Saturnian level of consciousness is 2,364$\frac{1}{2}$ times more Evolved than the secondary Saturnian level of consciousness.

From this numerical comparison, some small idea of the difference between these levels of consciousness can be seen and appreciated by the student.

That the real Spiritual worker is progressing slowly but surely towards an elevated goal, has been known for centuries. But only now, has a more complete and fuller picture of that goal been shown to him, so that he might be fired with a greater determination to reach out towards this, his eventual destination. The text of *The Nine Freedoms* goes much further than any occult or religious philosophy has ever gone. It penetrates thousands of lives into the future, beyond the Buddhist conception of Nirvana and gives definite and logical meaning to the vague orthodox Christian idea of: "ascending into Heaven."

"Take this into the silence with you. You will be better when you come out of it."

Indeed, no truer nor more sound advice has ever been given to the Metaphysical student. But, to repeat, the degree of improvement you will bring about within yourself is dependent upon your own efforts, dependent entirely upon the amount of energy you wish to expend, in order to bring this progressive improvement about within yourself and indeed within the lives of all those you come into contact with, either mentally through Prayer or physically through numerous other forms of definite Service.

AUTHOR'S RECOMMENDATIONS

NOTE 1. Read "The Initiation Of Earth," in *You Are Responsible!* (pages 145-159) and "The New World," in *Cosmic Voice* Issue No. 23 (pages 23-26) for further statements by Higher Authority regarding the inevitable Cosmic Initiation of Earth.

NOTE 2. A study of *Life On The Planets*, will reveal further information about Saturnian Intelligences.

NOTE 3. *Control Of The Vital Life Fluid*, is a practical Metaphysical lesson upon a subject of the uttermost importance to all really serious students of practical Metaphysics.

The above books and lessons are available from the publishers of *The Nine Freedoms*.

CHAPTER 9

THE NINTH FREEDOM WILL BE SOLAR EXISTENCE

SAINT GOO-LING

"By Power vested in Me, I Bless this Prasad in sacrifice to Brahma.

"Afterwards dispense to all.

"Now, today you will be given The Ninth Freedom. Afterwards, you will be given little Cross which will be Charged by Master Jesus. Take this little Cross into your Holy Place and when you are depleted, allow these radiations to charge you, which they will. They will charge you through heart and Christ Centres, so that you will have greater Wisdom.

"Do not let anyone touch these except yourself, for really Holy and Sacred.

"Do not forget that acceptance of these little Crosses also makes you a disciple of the Great Master Jesus, so that you must always behave in the manner befitting a disciple, to spread His Message and also, the Message of the Cosmic Masters, throughout the land.

"I go."

MARS SECTOR 6

"This is Mars Sector 6 reporting from Satellite No. 3, now in Magnetization Orbit—Terra, during Special Power Manipulation, prior to the correct delivery of The Ninth Freedom.

"The Ninth Freedom will be—SOLAR EXISTENCE.

"After a successful term of office as one of the Perfects of Saturn, the Cosmic Adept then moves to even a higher plane of existence. But, before this time, It travels to the Central Sun of this Galaxy for advanced Initiation into the secrets of Variable Dimension.

"After this Initiation, the Cosmic Adept then divorces Itself completely and retires into Meditation for a period which, in terrestrial years, would be 90,000.

"It then comes out of this deep Samadhic condition of Galactic Consciousness and practises the Seven Aspects of the White Magic of Continuance.

"After this successful practice, It again divorces Itself from all other Intelligences and It goeth again into Galactic Consciousness for a period of 500,000 of your terrestrial years.

"After this stage, It then returns again to the Central Sun for even another Initiation into the Three Aspects of Creative Magic. It cometh out and practises this.

"During this time, It can cause Itself to be divided into 3,100 parts and inhabit each part, whether it be human or animal, at the same time. It knows, consciously, what experience each part is passing through and can remotely control that part to bring about a definite, predetermined result.

"Then It is born through the most Sacred, Holy Flame in the Solar System—a Flame greater than anything individual. A Flame which is all collective, all powerful, all radiant. A Flame which is creative—for it is the Flame of the Solar Logos.

"Then It enters through the Flame and becomes One of the great Hierarchical Lords—One of the Lesser Planetary Lords.

"It hath no sex—for It hath all.

"It can control mind and matter within forty-nine dimensions. It loses even what individuality It had, by entering a state of Galactic Consciousness.

"Together They blend, to form—the mighty Sun. Not the essential Life of the Sun, but Its very radiations.

"This is total Freedom, as far as this Solar System is concerned, because it is, to some extent, greater limitation than any can realize.

"Together as the One, They work, radiating Power and energy to all lifestreams in the Solar System, radiating the very Power of Their bodies—the very energy of Their hearts.

"It is little wonder that the scribes who wrote the Bible regarded the Sun as God. It is little wonder that even in more ancient times than this, they worshipped this as a God, for deep, deep down, beneath the slime of man's ignorance, there was a burning Spark of the Divine, which burned with the selfsame Flame as burneth this mighty Globe.

"All the energy that terrestrial man uses comes from the Many, acting as the One.

"Think twice, oh man, before you use this energy wrongly. Know that if you attempt to use this energy wrongly, indeed you are committing a base crime.

"Let realization of The Ninth Freedom burn like an all-existing Flame into your very consciousness and govern each thought and action in accordance with the mightiness of This, the greatness of This, the undescribable beauty of This, the sacrifice of This, the Holiness of This, the simpleness of This.

"For the Many become the One in the Ninth Step. And in Their becoming, They practise, with every thought—aye, and with every etheric breath—Service to all.

"The great subtlety of Galactic Existence is realized by these Ones, Who look towards Their Illuminator and Teacher, namely, the Solar Logos—Itself—with reverence which cannot be described.

"They worship not This as The Absolute—but They see that This is a reflection of The Absolute Itself—and as such, is Sacred.

"So They join to help throughout the mighty Galactic System; aye, and even beyond stretches Their influence, Their help, Their guidance, Their heat, Their radiations, Their Power, Their Wisdom and Their Love. For we are told that we know not what Love be until we enter the gates of the Sun in lasting Service for all.

"In comparison with Their greatness, we are all but specks of Cosmic dust, floating in some magnetic stream, with vague, half-risen consciousness.

"It is strange to regard ourselves and think that there will come a day when we will enter this mighty portal. When we make such an observation, surely—surely, we can but become even more amazed at the great and lasting Glory of the God, Which made it all.

"Through the Freedoms you come, choosing your own time—be it fast, or slow. But, through these gates you must come.

"I, Mars Sector 6, do state upon Divine Authority, that you cannot miss these portals, no matter who you be. The Buddhas, the Jesuses, the Aetheriuses, the Kumaras, have at one time traveled this road; are now traveling it upon Their respective Planets; are traveling towards the Ninth Door.

"There is no possible description which could do half justice to the radiant beauty of the combined Lords of the Sun, for They shineth like veritable jewels around the waist of the Lords of Creation—for They help the mighty Lords of Creation to energize the Solar System, so that all lifestreams may have the great chance to enter the Ninth Door.

"Walk ye straight, oh men of Terra, if ye be wise. Nor step ye this side, neither the other—but go ye on and up, through the Eight Freedoms and into the Heart of God—in the Ninth.

"The Nine Freedoms have been given to Terra at this time, in order to stimulate and raise the consciousness of the few thinkers. Use this information well, for it will change you. For it will cause multitudinous thoughts to come into your mind. For this information will be the dawning of Wisdom for you.

"Use it well, oh brothers, Use it well.

"Relate Nim Seven Zero."

JESUS—LORD OF GRACE

THE MASTER JESUS

"Oh, my adorable children, I give you all my Love. I give you all my Blessings, now. May you be made strong. May you be guided upon your path.

"Oh, my children, know that you are not alone in your struggles. You can turn to us for help and guidance—for our Love."

The Master held up one of the wooden Crosses.

"This is not the symbol of crucifixion. It is the symbol of Resurrection into the mighty light of Ascension—into the Godhead. Regard it always, as such.

"Dwell ye not among those who hide from their followers the Truth of my coming. Pray for them; but dwell ye not in their house, for verily, when the Truth dawns, it will be as bitter as gall to them.

"I, Jesus, do Bless this Cross. I do Bless all of these as symbols of Resurrection. Take them, oh my children, with my Love—with my Blessings, to your hearts and you will find that, when you need it most, the Power—gentle, subtle and yet strong—will come from them unto you.

"Go you all forth with my Love and Blessings.

"Oh, Divine Everlasting God.

"Let Your Light shine upon all the people on Earth—Now.

"Let this Light enter into their hearts and minds—Now.

"So that they may realize their nearness,

"To the everlasting Flame which is—Thy Love.

"Bless you all. Bless you. May your journey through your Karma be a wonderful one. Bless you.

"Go with God."

THE TEXT IS CONCLUDED

MARS SECTOR 6

"This is Mars Sector 6 reporting from Satellite No. 3, now in Magnetization Orbit—Terra, during Magnetization Period No. 1, present phase.

"We were, of course, fully prepared for the gross interference by the dark forces, which was specifically designed to stop our Power Manipulation. You can see how we dealt with it—with success.

"During that Power Manipulation, terrestrials were used as channels so that energy from Satellite No. 3 could be radiated throughout Terra. Mental Channel No. 1 was also used so that energy could cause transmutation in certain places.

"During the next Magnetization Period of Terra, great energies will be sent out throughout the whole world. During this present Magnetization Period, energies must also be sent out throughout the world. Cooperate as much as you can.

"Demonstrate your belief in God by Service in this and other ways. Demonstrate your belief in God through the dispensation of your true Love. If you do this, you will prove that you are ready to climb the ladder from the pit of rebirth upon your Earth.

"Yet, be ye humble, for egotism is a disease. Cure it, oh terrestrials and go ye forth into The Nine Freedoms.

"Divorce all terrestrial screening. Balance all terrestrial units. Divorce screening from Mental Channel No. 1.

"All Transmissions now discontinued."

Delivered on Wednesday, March 15th, 1961.

SOLAR EXISTENCE

"Take this little Cross into your Holy Place and when you are depleted, allow these radiations to charge you, which they will. They will charge you through heart and Christ Centre, so that you will have greater Wisdom."

The reference here was made by Saint Goo-Ling to the small wooden Crosses which the Society had procured on definite instructions, one for each Member who attended. You will read later in this chapter how they were charged by the Master Jesus, but it is interesting to note here that, for the first time, some information regarding the type of Power to be put into the Crosses was given by Saint Goo-Ling. Although the Crosses were made of plain wood, they were, after being charged by the Master Jesus, turned into small batteries of Spiritual Power. The Metaphysical explanation for this feat is relatively simple. Everything that you physically touch is changed, because you have left a strong energy pattern in the article. With reference to the Crosses it must be remembered that, even though wood appears to be made up of atoms of substance packed very tightly together, there are nevertheless more spaces in the wood than there are particles of physical matter. An atom is rather like a Solar System, constructed of particles of matter which revolve around one or several protons, rather as Planets revolve around the Sun in this Solar System. If it were possible to enlarge an atom into astronomical proportions, we would have something similar to a Solar System with several particles of material revolving, at high velocity, around a central core and like the Solar System, there would be a great space or distance between each particle of material. Now, it is a known fact that man is not only a receiving, but also a transmitting apparatus. When he makes an intimate contact with a material object there is an interchange of subtle forces between the two. Not only does he take subtle energy away from the object he touches, but he also implants into it a complete pattern of his whole character. This implantation does not cause any change in the atomic structure of the article, even though the object contains a pattern which it did not possess before, but rather causes a change in the etheric spaces between the particles of matter which make up the object. It should be remembered, that the substance called Ether, flows freely through the sub-atomic spaces and indeed forms the vehicle in which the particles of matter making up atomic structure continually revolve. This Ether substance is highly mutable and transmutable. It can be molded into many thousands of different forms. It can be impressed with multitudinous energy patterns.

When the Master Jesus took up, in this case by proxy operating as He was through the author, one of these little Crosses to charge it, He impressed within the etheric spaces of the atomic structure of that object, the whole of His thought and energy pattern. He impressed it so strongly that, not only would the Ether retain this pattern, but would also give it up when, it was drawn upon by the need of the people who used this tiny Spiritual battery correctly. In the text, Saint Goo-Ling infers that the energy is of such a high vibrational quality that it will affect the heart and Christ Centres of all the people who have been given these Crosses. In other words, the energy put into the Spiritual battery by the Master Jesus could be drawn on by those who, with the right motive, made a request that this energy pattern come forth. The Cross, after being charged, was rather like a flash-lamp battery, which had an electrical charge induced into its chemical make up. When it is connected up to a light bulb in the right way and a switch pushed on so as to make the electric circuit complete, the bulb lights up.

The Cross was similar to this, constituted of certain chemical materials, containing a thought pattern put into the etheric spaces between the particles of matter by the Master Jesus. When this energy was needed, it could be connected up, in this case mentally by request or Prayer of the owner and it would, rather like the flashlamp battery, release this energy when polarized in the correct manner. We have here a good illustration of the action of Primary Energy which is completely answerable to mind. The mind of the owner forms a request built out of his or her particular need. This exerts a magnetic pull which causes the energy in the Cross to flow into the user, making its entry through the heart and Christ Centres, thereby causing a stimulation of the higher mental faculties.

It is interesting to note that such a Spiritual battery is never discharged, because the more it is used the higher its charge becomes. It was as though Jesus, when He charged these Crosses, brought into being certain paths through the Ether along which His Spiritual Power could flow. These were focused in the Cross to such an extent that, whenever the energy was withdrawn by the mental need of the owner, more would flow along the etheric paths impressed by Jesus, making the charged Cross a radiant battery of everlasting Spiritual Power.

The people who were privileged to attend The Nine Freedoms and were given one of these Crosses were indeed among the most fortunate people on Earth, as here was a prize seldom offered to any man. A priceless gift which could be given because the author had made a very definite request that Jesus should charge these Crosses. The correct occult ritual performed by the author, coupled with the general Karmic pattern of the attendees, after certain manipulations had been performed, allowed this request to be granted

"Do not let anyone touch these except yourself, for really Holy and Sacred."

It seems obvious why this should be so. If the Crosses fell into the wrong hands they would be so contaminated that they would cease to function correctly and in the way which was intended. When a particular person receives in his care an article which has been charged by a Master, he should see to it that no one else even touches the article—never mind uses it. If the Cross had not been given to the person who tried to use it, even though inspired with the right intention and purpose, it would be considerably less effective and his attempted use would be classed as a contamination.

"Do not forget that acceptance of these little Crosses also makes you a disciple of the Great Master Jesus, so that you must always behave in a manner befitting a disciple, to spread His Message and also, the Message of the Cosmic Masters, throughout the land."

Here Saint Goo-Ling reminded people, that not only were they offered something rare in the Universe, but also that this gift carried with it a definite responsibility. They could either accept this Cross or refuse it, whichever they wished. But their acceptance signified that they were forever SWORN into the true Service of the Master Jesus and other Cosmic Masters. No one can ever take a Blessing such as this, from a Master, without having to accept the grave responsibilities which go with such an Initiation. The people who chose to accept these charged Crosses were informed of this before their acceptance of the Holy Crosses, and it is hoped that they will never forget this unique happening, and that they will continue always to spread the correct teachings of Jesus and also the true teachings of the other Cosmic Masters, remaining always and forever faithful to the cause of

182 The Nine Freedoms

Truth. In this way, they were given an outstanding opportunity to balance their Karma in such a manner, that in future lives they could progress even more surely than they have done in this.

In a previous chapter it was pointed out that one can either choose Service to God through the right organization or try to carry on alone. The people who were invited to The Nine Freedoms had chosen their path of Service through The Aetherius Society and this was some reward for their choice.

It is worthy of mention that this was the second dispensation of Blessed Crosses by the Master Jesus to Members of The Aetherius Society. The first took place in England, after Jesus had delivered his New Age Bible, *The Twelve Blessings*. There are many Members in other parts who fervently pray that another similar wonderful mystical happening will take place so that next time they may be among the chosen ones.

"This is Mars Sector 6 reporting from Satellite No. 3, now in Magnetization Orbit—Terra, during a Special Power Manipulation, prior to the correct delivery of The Ninth Freedom."

You will read at the end of Chapter 4, a description of the operation of Satellite No. 3, which was still in orbit of Earth as The Ninth Freedom was given.

Before The Ninth Freedom could be delivered, however, there had to be a very Special Power Manipulation by the Master from Satellite No. 3, in order to transmute a very direct and concerted attack by the dark forces, inhabiting the lower astral realms, who tried their very hardest to stop this great Truth from being given to Earth.

While you should not dwell on evil, you cannot fight it effectively unless you can recognize it. There is no doubt that the dark forces scheme and plot to cause division and upset in the world, and the more you strive for Spiritual attainment, the more they will try to hold you back. Although, in your practice, you will never come under such heavy attack as did the author just prior to the delivery of The Ninth Freedom, it would be expedient for all of you to make a study of the methods you can use to protect yourself and those close to you, from undue interference, so that you may proceed with your Spiritual studies unhampered by the lower realms (Note 1).

"The Ninth Freedom will be—SOLAR EXISTENCE.

"After a successful term of office as One of the Perfects of Saturn, the Cosmic Adept then moves to even a higher plane of existence. But, before this time, It travels to the Central Sun of this Galaxy for advanced Initiation into the secrets of Variable Dimension."

The Perfects of Saturn are those Who constitute the inner circle of the Cosmic Advisory Council and after They have served a stated term of office in this capacity, They are then ready for the next major step in Their Evolution. You will notice that the text refers to the Perfect as—*"It."* In other words, as you have already learned, They are perfectly balanced tri-sexual Beings in the highest possible sense, rather than either male or female.

"The Central Sun of this Galaxy," means the great invisible Sun around which this Galaxy moves in a continual orbit—a hub of the Galactic Wheel, as it were. The Central Sun of this Galaxy would, of course, be One of the Lords of Creation and no doubt invisible to the human physical eye, but very visible to the true "Eye" of an advanced Saturnian Intelligence.

"After this Initiation, the Cosmic Adept then divorces Itself completely and retires into Meditation for a period which, in terrestrial years, would be 90,000."

After the Initiation into the secrets of "Variable Dimension" on the Central Sun of the Galaxy, the Cosmic Adept then completely detaches Itself from all physical and mental contact with other Adepts and retires into another long period of Meditation, which the text refers to as: *"Galactic Consciousness."*

We do not have the slightest conception what kind of state Galactic Consciousness really is, but as Cosmic Consciousness, or the awareness of the inter-relationship of all things upon Earth, is the ultimate Meditative state upon this Earth, it is logical to assume that Galactic Consciousness must be the awareness, thousands of times more embracing or profound, of the inter-relationship of all things within not only one Planet or even a Solar System, but in a mighty Galaxy. Such a state is beyond our comprehensive abilities and can only be referred to as a possible existence, rather than something we have had the experience of living through.

"It then comes out of this deep Samadhic condition of Galactic Consciousness and practices the Seven Aspects of the White Magic

of Continuance."

By the reference here to the: *"White Magic of Continuance,"* it would appear that this is essentially rather a female type of magic, leaning rather more towards Preservation than Creation. The Intelligence learns how to preserve that which has already been brought into Creation. We will see later on in the text what is meant by this.

"After this successful practice, It again divorces Itself from all other Intelligences and It goeth again into Galactic Consciousness for a period of 500,000 of your terrestrial years. After this stage, It then returns again to the Central Sun for even another Initiation into the Three Aspects of Creative Magic. It cometh out and practises this."

Here we have even another return of the Lifestream into Galactic Consciousness, this time for a much longer period, equal to 500,000 terrestrial years. It is extremely difficult to imagine a period of Meditation lasting this long. In fact, it is more difficult for an advanced Metaphysician to grasp the depth of such Meditation, than it would be for an uninitiated aborigine to understand what a light terrestrial type of Meditation could possibly be like.

"The Three Aspects of Creative Magic," seems to be the positive male-type of magic of actual Creation—Itself. This does not mean to say that the Saturnian Adept is God, but an essential Agent for The Absolute working under Its direction, which of course is the plu-perfect, inevitable, irrevocable Law.

"During this time, It can cause Itself to be divided into 3,100 parts and inhabit each part, whether it be human or animal, at the same time. It knows, consciously, what experience each part is passing through and can remotely control that part to bring about a definite, predetermined result."

This is another reference to the amazing capabilities of the really advanced Cosmic Adept. Even before the final Initiation into the Sun, It is capable of feats beyond the wildest conception of even the most imaginative among us. It should also be noted that such a One would only split Its consciousness up into these many parts in order to bring about a very definite result; indeed the type of result which would be dictated by a complete working knowledge of the great Law of Creation and Preservation which is God. Of course, a Master of such calibre would never need a part of Its consciousness to be born as a child upon Earth, thus having to evolve from the child to the adult to bring about a desired result. Should anyone on Earth claim to be a part of the consciousness of a Sun-Being or even a Saturnian for that matter, then leave him entirely alone for you will know that he is the victim of gross, egotistical delusion. The genuine signpost to Truth not only shows you the right path to follow, but also that which is wrong.

It is true, as you have seen previously in this book, that certain Interplanetary Intelligences are introduced into the environmental conditions of Earth, in a terrestrial body and that a limited number are even born through the womb of an Earth woman, so that Their particular task may be performed at a later date (Note 3). Such a rare happening is really a Karmic manipulation, the reason for which has to be Meditated upon to be even partially understood. But this is a very different procedure from that which would be adopted by an elevated Being on the point of introduction into the foremost Creative point in this Solar System, namely the Sun. The tasks performed by such a Being would never need the Karmic manipulation which demanded such a birth as this. If it had to, for instance, introduce a part of Itself on to this Earth, It would introduce an adult form which may stay here for two seconds or maybe even some years and then leave. It would never need to manipulate Karma in the same way as an Interplanetary Intelligence may need to manipulate it. The very fact that the Interplanetary Intelligence very rarely has to adopt this method should prove that the higher Master never needs to perform the same tasks undertaken quite successfully by the pupil. This is a very important point and the reason why it has been stressed.

"Then It is born through the most Sacred Holy Flame in the Solar System—a Flame greater than anything individual. A Flame which is all collective, all powerful, all radiant. A Flame which is Creative—for It is the Flame of the Solar Logos."

What pitiful faltering words can do justice to this? The more such passages are read and even slightly understood, the more limitation is realized. Not even the greatest expression possible to man can ever begin to describe the ineffable, Divine beauty of the magnificent Lord of the Sun. We can only say simply, as would a little child: the reference here is made to the great Sun-Lord Itself. This is the Creative Flame through which the Lifestream has now won Its birth. Through experiences beyond our imagination, through suffering the depth of which we know not of and joy, the like of which we will not know for a million lives, It has won this supreme Initiation into the Sun Itself and It becomes, as the text later states, One of the Lesser Planetary Lords—the Greater Planetary Lords being the Planets—Themselves.

"It can control mind and matter within forty-nine dimensions. It loses even what individuality It had, by entering the state of Galactic Consciousness."

The forty-nine dimensions must be the seven dimensions upon each of the seven planes of existence. It is useless to even try to describe them, nobody could. The sum capability of even a Master's descriptive ability ends with the seven dimensions which the few know to exist. It would be utter foolishness to attempt any description of those dimensions upon the seven higher planes which, in theory if not in realization, we believe do exist.

"Together They blend to form—the Mighty Sun. Not the essential Life of the Sun, but Its very radiations."

The Sun is the most Holy Being in this Solar System.

It is the Being upon which we all depend, absolutely and completely, for our very existence, our very life, our very water, our very food, the very air we breathe, and the very Universal Life Forces which charge that air with life so that we might express and Evolve. When the Lifestream has passed through the Initiations of Galactic Consciousness, It blends together with other Lifestreams Who are ready and They work and act as one Being, as a Lesser Planetary Lord. So advanced are They that the next step higher along the Evolutionary scale would be an amalgamation together of several of such advanced Beings, which would result in the birth of the Logos of a Planet similar to Earth, Mars or Venus.

"Together as the One, They work, radiating Power and energy to all lifestreams in the Solar System, radiating the very Power of Their Bodies—the very energy of Their Hearts."

Your body is solidified sunlight. Everything you see, smell, hear, taste or touch on this Earth, is solidified sunlight. Even the great Universal Life Forces or Pranas, around which all Creation revolves throughout the Planetary system, are sunlight on one energy plane or another. A moment's reflection on this will give you the realization that this is indeed one of the greatest Truths of Metaphysics.

The Lifestreams, blending together, continually radiate Power to all lifestreams in this Solar System, continually send the great Creative WORD, the A-U-M, through the Ethers every 32 minutes of every hour of every day, week, month, year, cycle and every millennium.

From the Sun came the Planets in this Solar System and when Their present Life is finished, back to the Sun again They will go. The Beings on the Sun are radiating the essence of Their very Bodies through the Ethers, so that life in this Solar System might use this energy in order to express itself in multitudinous ways, in order to gain experience, in order to Evolve, in order to continue the journey back to the Divine Source again. If ever there is such a thing as a debt, then we are in debt forever to such Beings as Those on the Sun. Never can we hope to repay such a debt, save by a cancellation through some aspect of Karmic Law, if that is possible. The very energy from Their Bodies gives us the Universal Life Force which makes up our food, water and air we breathe. The very energy of Their Hearts gives us our highest inspirations, our purest Love. The great tides of Spiritual energy which continually flow like mighty seas through this Solar System, upon which all life is entirely dependent, is the very blood of These ineffable Beings. There is not even a rock which could live in its present form, except by the mercy and Creative ability of these Great Masters. If ever life on Earth was dependent upon any one thing, THEN IT IS COMPLETELY AND ABSOLUTELY DEPENDENT UPON THE SUN FOR ITS EVERY EXPRESSION.

If you forget everything else in the world, it will pay you always to remember this.

"It is little wonder that the scribes who wrote the Bible regarded the Sun as God. It is little wonder that even in more ancient times than this, they worshipped this as a God—for deep deep down beneath the slime of man's ignorance, there was a burning Spark of the Divine which burned with the selfsame Flame as burneth this mighty Globe."

It might come as a shock to many of you to learn that the God of the Bible is the Sun; but it is so. Your Meditations will tell you beyond any doubt that it is so. The WORD which was with God in the beginning of this Solar System was the Creative sound A-U-M. This Creative resonance was sent forth by the most Ancient Being in this system—

the Sun. In deep Meditation you can tune into this old, yet most modern Creative sound as it pervades the Super-Conscious mind belt of Earth. Once you have heard the one Creative sound vibration, penetrating deep through the heart of all things, you will KNOW that these words are the burning and everlasting Truth. The nearest thing to God in this Solar System is the Sun. We cannot conceive of anything greater than this, for it would be beyond the capabilities of our awareness. Throughout the centuries man has looked into the face of the Sun and oftimes, without even realizing it, has worshipped God through this nearest aspect of It.

"All the energy that terrestrial man uses comes from the Many, acting as the One. Think twice, oh man, before you use this energy wrongly. Know that if you attempt to use it wrongly, indeed you are committing a base crime."

If all men would realize that they are absolutely responsible for every unit of energy they use, then indeed the world would change overnight. Every wrong thought and wrong action is Spiritual energy debased, and those responsible only involve themselves. There will come a time of reckoning, when they will have to bear the direct Karma for misusing this Sacred and Divine Energy, of this there is not the slightest doubt. Such people should have our most fervent Prayers, because Karma, although not cruel, is entirely just. What limitations Karma will impose upon the "hitlers," the "attillas," the "napoleons," the war-starters and the users of the evil hydrogen bomb, only the Lords of Karma know, but such people are not in an enviable position to say the very least.

As stated previously man has one sure ability, he can manipulate his own Karma. If he regards every unit of energy as Sacred and Divine, using this for the benefit of all, then indeed, does such a one manipulate his Karmic pattern so that in future lives he is given even a greater chance to use more energy in even a more beneficial manner.

The text continues to describe the wonderful Beings, Who amalgamate together to work under the strict directives of the Solar Logos, Which is One of the Lords of Creation, so that They may help the great plan of Evolution to work out. No simple words can add anything to this description. Read this part of the text again—you will agree.

"I, Mars Sector 6, do state upon Divine Authority that you can-

not miss these portals, no matter who you be. The Buddhas, the Jesuses, the Aetheriuses, the Kumaras, have at one time travelled this road; are now travelling it upon Their respective Planets; are travelling towards the Ninth Door."

This is a very definite statement and one which, whether believed or liked, cannot ever be altered or erased for it is now written forever in the Akashic Records of Earth! Mars Sector 6 has been given "Divine Authority," to give to the Earth its greatest occult Truth. When a Master of this calibre claims: "Divine Authority," you may depend upon it that such Authority has been granted. Beings of His status do not play fast and loose with words as we blind children so often do upon Earth. No matter who you are, you must travel through these particular Initiations before you can enter the Ninth Door, or enjoy The Ninth Freedom as one of the Lesser Planetary Lords, leading to eventual amalgamation into the Sun Itself. This is the gospel Truth and as it is, sooner or later, you will all have to make this journey. You can start it as soon as you choose. The Divine promise has been given to each and every one of you. IT IS UP TO YOU WHEN YOU WILL TAKE IT, NOT WHETHER YOU WILL TAKE IT!

"The Nine Freedoms have been given to Terra at this time in order to stimulate and raise the consciousness of the few thinkers. Use this information well, for it will change you. For it will cause multitudinous thoughts to come into your mind. For this information will be as the dawning of Wisdom for you. Use it well, oh brothers. Use it well."

The profound effect caused in the lives of some people who attended lectures on The Nine Freedoms has to be seen to be believed. If such an effect, for good, can be brought about by the spoken word, even a greater result can be brought about by a careful study of the text within this book as, unlike the spoken word, the written word can be studied and analyzed over and over again. Even up to now, it has been noticed, with the lectures on this work, that a rise of consciousness has been brought about in all those who have been exposed to The Nine Freedoms.

The text states: *"Your internal vibrations have been altered by these utterances."*

It must be so. Here we have, FOR THE FIRST TIME IN METAPHYSICAL OR PHYSICAL HISTORY, a definite path which we will all take through Evolution. Before the delivery of The Nine Freedoms, man's Evolution was said to end in some vague, undefined place called "Heaven," with no attempt whatsoever to give this destination any Metaphysical meaning. Or, in the case of the Buddhist, the destination was a state of consciousness called "Nirvana," again without an adequate explanation of its Metaphysical significance. Now, for the very first time, a definite course has been given to mankind through his future Evolution. This fact alone will cause a pronounced change, a dawning of true Wisdom within the heart and mind of the really serious student. After all, this work has been prepared for the serious student, not just for those who may read for intellectual stimulation.

In The Nine Freedoms, you have been given many pointers which will act as a framework for your concentration, contemplation and at a later date, your Meditation. You have been told many things that you can take into the silence with you, so that you can come out of it a different, more Enlightened, more aware person, vibrating with a fuller, more complete appreciation of the interrelationship and balance of all things. It is KNOWN that this book will bring about such wonderful results in the lives of many students. As this is so, all the work which went into its preparation has not been in vain.

JESUS—THE LORD OF GRACE

"Oh my children, know that you are not alone in your struggles. You can turn to us for help and guidance—for our Love."

The Master Jesus, by making this statement, did not mean that He is attendant on you to solve your personal difficulties or to give you personal messages. A Master of this calibre never has, neither will He ever, give to you nor anyone else, a purely personal message. But what He did mean was that every step that you take decisively towards an understanding of and adherence to the Law, the Cosmic Hierarchy will take an equivalent step towards you. In many ways will the true seeker be helped and guided along the path to Truth.

You can better understand this statement of the Master Jesus by studying and practising, "The Twelve Blessings," as given by Jesus. This will give you a more acute awareness and a deeper appreciation of the wholeness of all things, as well as, and this is vitally important, help you to become more vibrant, so that you can be of even greater Service to the world as a whole and to yourself through this essential Service (Note 2).

"This is not the symbol of crucifixion. It is the symbol of Resurrection into the mighty light of Ascension—into the Godhead. Regard it always, as such."

When the Master Jesus said this, He was referring to one of the small Crosses He was Blessing. For thousands of years the orthodox Christian Religion has pinned Jesus upon the cross, using it as a frightful, nightmarish apparatus of defeat. It should be known that this Being came from the Planet Venus. That the Star of Bethlehem was a shining Spacecraft which actually came from the Planet Saturn. That the Masters of Saturn manipulated the virgin birth of the Venusian, Jesus, upon this Earth. That He came for two reasons, in this order of importance. The first to die. The second to give a code of morals and ethics to mankind.

That He died and died horribly, all Christians believe. It is pitiful though, that orthodoxy does not teach correctly why His death was necessary.

In those days, a violent terrestrial catastrophe was due. The Solar Hierarchy saw fit to effect a Divine intervention. They did so by bringing a volunteer from the Planet Venus to be born in a terrestrial body upon Earth, who would later be murdered so that by His sacrifice the catastrophe, due in those days, could be offset. Jesus did not die to forgive anyone of you your sins. This would be a Karmic impossibility. But He did die in order to offset an awful catastrophe, so that all lifestreams upon Earth could continue their Evolution, unimpeded by the setback which would have been caused had this terrible cataclysm been allowed. Because of this sacrificial act upon the altar of true Service, everyone on Earth is forever indebted to the Interplanetary Saviour—Jesus.

There is no doubt in the mind of thinking man that had Jesus, the wonderful Venusian, wished to forestall His murder, He could have done so. The ignorant, uncouth, unthinking, unwashed rabble who crucified Jesus, or the vile black magicians who goaded them on, could not have laid one of their dirty hands upon Him had He but raised His little finger to stop them. But He knew that He had come to be sacrificed in this manner. He also knew that by His very death, He would be as a living proof of Ascension to all men.

He died in a physical terrestrial body and yet, three days later, He Ascended in a body of great Light and came before His followers, made whole again.

Metaphysically what the Avatar did was this: He left the physical body when it had been so mutilated upon the cross as to be incapable of retaining life and then, when it was put in the crypt, He broke down the physical structure of His body, reformed it into a vehicle of finer matter and inhabited this body in full Life. That, dear readers, is what the Master means when He says: "The cross is a symbol of Resurrection."

Without His death, the world would have been in tremendous upheaval; you would not have been sitting down, studying as you are; your Evolution may have been held up for thousands of years; you would not have had the living proof before you of the Initiation of Ascension. Indeed is the cross the symbol of Resurrection. It is symbolic of Evolution through and above the base physical, of having complete Mastery over the lower orders of energy through superb demonstration. The results of His demonstration were predetermined and every move was carefully mapped out before Jesus ever came to Earth and whosoever says otherwise cannot think beyond pure basic materialism.

As well as performing this great Metaphysical feat, Jesus, the Master from Venus, Who was delivered to this Earth in an Interplanetary Satellite, which came from Saturn, gave unto man the secret of using the greatest Power known on Earth—the Power of pure Love. As though His supreme sacrifice were not enough, as though saving the Earth from devastating catastrophe were not enough, He went even further and instructed you in the correct use of the Holy Power, the vibrant energy, the essence of the very Heart of the Solar Logos, to raise not only yourself but all things around you. Never before had such a pronounced demonstration of the Metaphysical use of the energy called—Love, been given. But alas, it seems that the world has forgotten the very essence of His teachings. It seems that the world, on the whole, feeling its inferiority, its insecurity, has thrown the wealth of its mind and matter into making bigger and more deadly weapons. That it has started to explore Space, not so much to give freely any benefits from such exploration to the whole of humanity, but more as a type of escapism from its own dark past, escapism from the insecurities of a future made uncertain by possession, avarice and materialistic worship.

Even so, that noble Saint of Grace and Purity, Who hung upon the cross of Golgotha, did not do so in vain, for He left behind a Light which no military mind can ever stamp out, which no dictator can ever extinguish. He left a sure Flame burning in the hearts of true men upon Earth, a Light which, sooner or later, will break into a magnificent Spiritual Fire to transmute the murderous atom bomb and consume the throne of dictatorship upon which sits the self pronounced, atheistic communist who unsuccessfully tries, in many devious ways, to squash belief in this wondrous Being—the Lord Jesus.

"Dwell ye not among those who hide from their followers the Truth of my coming. Pray for them; but dwell ye not in their house, for verily, when the Truth dawns, it will be as bitter as gall to them."

"The Truth of my coming," the Truth that He came from another Planet, that He came to manipulate Karma for you. That He came, not as the one and only son of God, to make any false promise to you, to say that if you believe in Him, then your sins are washed away and that you are immediately free to do as you wish; but the Truth that Jesus came to help you, to guide you, to save you from a catastrophe so that you may continue your journey through Evolution. This is what Jesus means in the statement.

Another Truth which He came to show was how wrong it is to kill, murder, thieve and lie. Keep away from those who tell you otherwise, whoever they may be, whatever position they may hold, for they are going against the Word as spoken by the Lord Jesus—shining Prince of God's Peace.

After giving wonderful advice to all, He then Blessed all the Crosses in the way which has been detailed previously.

"Oh Divine Everlasting God,
"Let Your Light shine upon all the peoples of the Earth—Now.
"Let this Light enter into their hearts and minds—Now.
"So that they may realize their nearness to the everlasting Flame which is—Thy Love."

This wonderful Prayer can and should be used by all serious students. It was spoken thus by Jesus so that all would use it in Prayer for the world as a whole. At the end of this book you will see two more wonderful Prayers given by Jesus. Use those too in the ways which have been described and you will be well armed and fortified by your constant use of these, correctly balanced, unselfish Prayers.

THE TEXT IS CONCLUDED

"We were, of course, fully prepared for the gross interference by the dark forces which was specifically designed to stop our Power Manipulation. You can see how we dealt with it—with success."

The Cosmic Master, Mars Sector 6, is referring here to the heavy attack upon the author at the beginning of The Ninth Freedom, as previously stated. This attempted set-back was dealt with by a very advanced Power Manipulation which not only transmuted the attack by the lower astral entities, but also released tremendous Spiritual energy to the world as a whole. See the graph at the end of Chapter 4.

"During that Power Manipulation, terrestrials were used as channels so that energy from Satellite No. 3 could be radiated throughout Terra. Mental Channel No. 1 was also used so that energy could cause transmutation in certain places."

The reference to terrestrials here means not only those Members of The Aetherius Society invited to listen to The Nine Freedoms, but also other cooperators throughout the world who held mystical Prayer circles at the exact time each Freedom was delivered.

"Mental Channel No. 1," refers to the author.

"During the next Magnetization Period of Terra, great energies will be sent throughout the whole world. During this present Magnetization Period, energies must also be sent throughout the world. Cooperate as much as you can."

This is an appeal to all people to cooperate with the tremendous tides of Spiritual energies which are radiated from Satellite No. 3 when it is in orbit of this Earth. Fuller particulars of the orbital sequence of Satellite No. 3 are published in Aetherius Society material, when these are announced by the Masters.

"Demonstrate your belief in God by Service in this and other ways."

During the time that Satellite No. 3 is in orbit of this Earth, concentrated Spiritual energy is radiated through those people who cooperate and use these energies for the benefit of all men. This is counted as a very potent act of Service. If you pray during this time, your Prayers are enhanced 3,000 times. This means that, if you say a

Prayer at a normal time, you release from point A—yourself, to point B—the destination of your Prayer, x-units of energy. When the Satellite is in orbit of this Earth, if you give that same Prayer in the same place, in the same way, for the same reason, if it is a Spiritual one, you will release from point A—yourself, to point B—the destination of your Prayer, 3,000 x-units of energy. That is why Prayer is so essential during the time the Satellite is in orbit of this Earth. You can make a practical demonstration of your belief in God by praying for world Peace and Enlightenment at all times, but especially during this Holy Time, or the time when the Satellite is allowed to come into orbit of this Earth by Divine Authority (Note 4).

"Demonstrate your belief in God through the dispensation of your true Love. If you do this, you will prove that you are ready to climb the ladder from the pit of rebirth upon your Earth."

Please note, that the text states: *"through the dispensation of your true Love,"* not by man's excuse for love, but by the radiation of true Love, can man show his belief in a Divine Source. You can truly Love all things and all people, and you should do so, even though you may not like them. Love is not a way to bind and possess, but a way to free. It is not an expression of emotion, but mental energy transmuted on to the highest possible level. This is true Love. It is not personalized, it is universal. It is not binding, but gives Freedom. Pure Love has great Healing Powers, it is the one force in the Cosmic system which can multiply itself from itself. The man who uses true Love is the wise man, for Wisdom is Love in action.

"Yet be ye humble, for egotism is a disease. Cure it, oh terrestrials, and go ye forth into The Nine Freedoms."

The last piece of valuable advice given to you in The Nine Freedoms is one of the most important aspects of behavior. How subtle is egotism. It builds the dictators. It makes the materialist say that we are alone in the System and the highest form of life in the Universe. Where does it spring from? Where else but from a hidden inferiority complex inherent within those who are incapable of lasting accomplishment. The Master states that egotism is a disease like a cancer which eats its way into the very brain of man and warps his outlook and his decisions. Egotism and materialism are evil twins which play together upon the shores of man's mind, causing turbulence and grief. If we cure this egotistical disease by our heightened awareness of the wonders of ever expanding Creation, we can go forward relieved from this limitation.

The last sentence in *The Nine Freedoms* is indeed an invaluable key we should all place firmly in the lock of our completely disciplined thought; turn it boldly, open the door and step forward into the essence of Truth—the Light of Freedom.

AUTHOR'S RECOMMENDATIONS

NOTE 1. Study of the Metaphysical lesson, *Psychic Self Defense,* will assist all students in methods of protection from interfering forces.
Study of The Conclusion and correct practice of the Sacred Prayers therein will also be a help towards protection from outside interference of all kinds.

NOTE 2. *The Twelve Blessings,* is the New Age Bible given by the Master Jesus. This consists of twelve mystic practices and Prayers designed to enhance the awareness of all who diligently practise them.

NOTE 3. One of the most significant revelations explaining the advanced Metaphysical procedure adopted by Interplanetary Intelligences who are introduced on to this Earth is given in the Metaphysical lesson, *The Four Aspects Of Creation.*

NOTE 4. The literature recommended at the end of Chapter 4 will give further information regarding the all important function of Satellite No. 3.

The above mentioned book and Metaphysical lessons are obtainable from the publishers of *The Nine Freedoms.*

THE CONCLUSION

DYNAMIC PRAYER BRINGS RESULTS

Prayer is an exact Metaphysical science and as such can be used to bring about quite outstanding results if it is applied correctly. We are all living in a world of energy vibrations, which, by the very nature of their Creation by the One Divine Source and their existence within the framework of manifestation, makes them inter-related one with another. This inter-relationship is governed by the one great Law of Karma—or if you prefer, the Law which makes action and reaction opposite and equal. As this is so, all our thoughts and actions take place within the framework of this all-pervasive, all regulating Law. What we send out, we get back, no more and no less.

If we transmit highly elevating energies of a Spiritual nature, then in return, we receive vibrant, uplifting and inspirational energies back from the never ending Universal Supply.

One of the simplest and surest ways to receive such powerful forces is by the transmission of similar forces released from within our higher selves through Dynamic Prayer.

To really guarantee results through Prayer, it is no good just paying lip service to the constant, unfeeling repetition of words, no matter how beautiful the prose may be. Prayer, to be effective, should be said with real feeling. When Jesus prayed, He put His whole Heart into it. We should all do the same. Whether we make up our own inspirational Prayers, or repeat those already given, we should put all our heart into them. Every vestige of our Love and feeling should be transmuted into each Prayer we perform so that the very essence of our highest Love energy is sent out in one continual, vibrant stream to every one. After our Prayer, we should have such faith that we will be able to detach ourselves completely from what we have just said and let the result come. This is the secret of Dynamic Prayer!

By sending outward, from ourselves, the higher energies, we must, sooner or later reap the rich Spiritual harvest of our actions according to the infallible Law of the Universe.

Stand with the feet slightly apart. Raise the hands, palms outwards and repeat the wonderful Prayers given to you by the Master Jesus.

Allow the energy to pour forth through you. Try to visualize this Power, as a radiant White Light, streaming forth from the heart centre and from the centres in the middle of the palm of each hand. Then you will find that Dynamic Prayer really does work.

The two following Prayers can be used regularly by active Metaphysical students whose earnest desire it is to really help all mankind as well as their own Karmic progress.

These two very powerful and Metaphysically balanced Prayers were delivered by the Master Jesus through the author of *The Nine Freedoms*.

The "Prayer For Spiritual Workers," has been in constant successful use since its first publication by the Society (Note 1). As you will see, this is specially designed by the Master Jesus as a Prayer for the upliftment of all Spiritual workers who are actively engaged in Service for humanity and the radiation of higher Powers to the world as a whole. The advice given by the Master Jesus, at the time of delivery, is also included so that all active students may gain the uttermost benefit from the continual use of this magnificent Prayer.

Already "The New Lord's Prayer" is well-known, having been previously published by The Aetherius Society (Note 2). The sound track of the actual delivery of this Prayer has been made into a disc by Columbia Recording Co. It is already being used by individuals and congregations alike, in many countries throughout the world with amazing results, which are constantly being vouched for by the users of this powerful Prayer.

The desperate need in the hearts of active Metaphysical students and that of the whole of mankind, for Spiritual Power and upliftment in this troubled age, has prompted the publishers to include these already well-proven Prayers as a fitting conclusion to *The Nine Freedoms*.

May God Bless your Spiritual efforts and your study of—*The Nine Freedoms*.

NOTE 1. "Prayer For Spiritual Workers," was first published on a tape recording called "Watch This Year." This is the complete sound track of a series of Transmissions from Cosmic Authorities which constitute an appeal to all Spiritual workers to unite in their efforts for world peace.

NOTE 2. See *Cosmic Voice*, Issue No. 26 (pages 21-28) for full particulars of the outstanding Cosmic Transmissions which preceded the delivery of "The New Lord's Prayer."

Obtainable from the publishers of *The Nine Freedoms*.

PRAYER FOR SPIRITUAL WORKERS

"Oh mighty God, I Bless all those
Who, because of their limitations,
Would smite me.

Oh mighty God, I Bless all those
Who, because of their weakness,
Would not heed me.

Oh mighty God, I Bless all those
Who, because of their ignorance,
Would defile You, through me.

And I ask, oh mighty God, oh Wondrous Power,
That Your Strength may be given to me now;
So that I might be fortified by this,
So that I might go forward bravely into the world,
And despite reception, send forth my Love of Thee,
Throughout all races of man.

Oh mighty God, give me the Power and strength,
To rise above my Karmic weakness,
The deficiencies in the pattern of my Evolution,
So that I might Evolve and become stronger,
Aye, and even stronger, in Thy Everlasting Light.
Oh God, Thy Will be done."

Delivered, December 22nd, 1962.   THE MASTER JESUS

THE MASTER ADVISES: "Say this Prayer with your heart and with your
Soul, when the world is cold to you—and you will be warmed. Say it
when you are down—and you will be lifted. Say it when you are alone—
and you will be comforted by a Presence. Say it when you fail—and you
will succeed. Say it when you die—and you will live. Say it so that you may
gain sufficient Power and strength to do greater things."

THE NEW LORD'S PRAYER

"Oh Divine and Wondrous Spirit!
Oh Everlasting Lord of Hosts!
Send forth, now, through me
Thy great and lasting Power.

Allow me, oh mighty God, the lasting privilege,
Of radiating to all the world Thy great Love,
So that those who suffer may be given the
Power and energy to rise above their weaknesses.

Oh mighty God, in great humility do I ask you
To send forth Your Power.
To give to me this great lasting privilege,
Of being a channel so that my suffering brothers
May be helped and guided and healed and
Lifted into Thy Light.
So that they who know not may look up,
And in doing so, receive through their Higher Selves,
Your Divine Counsel.

Oh mighty God, this day have you granted me,
A Divine privilege.
I ask you, now, to give to me the strength,
So that never again will I turn from my inner vision of you;
Om Shanti, Shanti, Shanti.

In praise of your Greatness, oh God,
Doth my Soul sing.
Grant it energy to sing on
Forever and forever."

Delivered, December 20th, 1961.   THE MASTER JESUS